W9-BMU-275

Milford Town Library
80 Spruce Street
Milford, MA 01757

WITHDRAWN

Leadership Transformed

Leadership Transformed

Dr. Peter Fuda

New Harvest
Houghton Mifflin Harcourt
BOSTON   NEW YORK
2013

Copyright © 2013 by Dr. Peter Fuda

All rights reserved

This edition published by special arrangement with Amazon Publishing

For information about permission to reproduce selections from this book,
write to Permissions, Houghton Mifflin Harcourt Publishing Company,
215 Park Avenue South, New York, New York 10003.

www.hmhbooks.com

Library of Congress Cataloging-in-Publication Data
Fuda, Peter.
Leadership transformed / Dr. Peter Fuda.
pages cm
"A New Harvest Book."
Includes bibliographical references and index.
ISBN 978-0-544-02693-3
1. Leadership. I. Title.
HD57.7.F8195 2013
658.4'092 — dc23   2013010185

Printed in the United States of America
DOC 10 9 8 7 6 5 4 3 2 1

For Kara and Bella, the fuel for my fire

Contents

Read This First

"Decades of academic analysis have given us more than 350
definitions of leadership. Literally thousands of empirical
investigations of leaders have been conducted in the last 75
years alone, but no clear and unequivocal understanding
exists as to what distinguishes leaders from non-leaders
and what distinguishes effective leaders from ineffective
leaders."

— WARREN BENNIS AND BURT NANUS

I STARTED THE DOCTORAL research that forms the back-
bone of hard data for this book on December 16, 2005. I can
be very precise about this date because it was the same day my
wife, Kara, gave birth to our daughter, Isabella—probably the
best excuse ever to leave early on the very first day of class. As
I sped toward the hospital, I had time to reflect on why, with a
new baby arriving and a rapidly growing consulting business, I
had just committed the next five years of my life to serious academic research.

Three things came to mind. First, I was really frustrated with
the leadership literature, as highlighted by Bennis and Nanus.

Second, I had an expedient (read: selfish) need to make sense of the "success" I was experiencing in my consulting practice. Third, I wanted to make a significant contribution to the field of leadership, in particular to our understanding of leadership transformation. By transformation, I mean the process by which an ordinary manager becomes an extraordinary leader.

As a committed student of leadership and somebody who had, over the course of twelve years, been fortunate enough to build a healthy business out of an obsession with the subject, I had become more and more frustrated with the literature. In my reading of both academic and practitioner-oriented texts, I struggled with the long lists of qualities and attributes that defined "effective" leadership, and with the heroic persona that was often attributed to the person sitting atop the organizational hierarchy. It wasn't that I had a problem with the content of these works — they espoused largely noble attributes like vision, courage, and integrity. The problem was that, after so many years of working very closely with CEOs and senior executives around the world, I had never met the superhero leader described in much of what I read.

Since 2001, the work of my consulting company, The Alignment Partnership (TAP), had been squarely focused on helping leaders transform themselves, their leadership teams, and their organizations. Unlike the ideal leaders presented in the books I was reading, the leaders I was working with were mere mortals doing the best they could under ever-increasing pressure. The question I had personally become obsessed with was "What does it take for an ineffective leader to transform into a highly effective leader?" I was searching for a substantive work to support and accelerate my own efforts, a work that laid out a clear road map for transformation in leaders.

Meanwhile, I was personally witnessing transformations unfold quite frequently. Over our first five years in business, my company had grown in stature and reputation following our publication of case studies of success in multinational companies like MasterCard, Bayer, and Dun & Bradstreet, and in the public sector with the government of Hong Kong. In fact, by 2005 we had a dozen case studies of organizational transformation, and more than a hundred stories of leadership transformation involving CEOs and senior executives. As a result, I was already feeling friendly pressure from the consulting community, the business media, and academia to disclose our "transformation formula."

This attention was flattering but, given the often-quoted statistic that more than 70 percent of all change efforts end in failure, not entirely surprising. It was also very uncomfortable for me, mostly because I had little idea how to respond. I could describe the tools and frameworks we used and the interventions we ran, but that felt superficial, especially since many of these elements were widely used by consultants around the world. To paraphrase Karl Weick, we can only make sense of life retrospectively, even though it must be lived prospectively. It was time to make sense of our past in order to inform our future.

All through my academic research, I held on to the hope that my results would help me make sense of our work, and eventually allow me to establish and refine processes that would improve our practice. I would then share those insights with leaders and consultants around the world across a range of platforms, from management journals to speaking engagements to, perhaps, a book.

Along with my supervising professor, Richard Badham, and my research assistant, Skye Phillips, my big dream was to produce a work of sufficient quality that it could be published in the *Harvard Business Review*, a journal I had read religiously every month for some fifteen years. In November 2011, this dream came true when *HBR* published "Fire, Snowball, Mask, Movie: How Leaders Spark and Sustain Change," based on our research findings. This outcome further encouraged me to share our insights in greater depth in a book-length work—the one you are holding right now.

As we were shaping our approach to the research, Richard and I had the good fortune to speak with leadership guru Manfred Kets de Vries following a lecture he gave in 2006. We asked him what model he used in his leadership transformation initiatives, and he admitted that he acted as a *bricoleur*, one who selects, mixes, and adapts his materials in an iterative process of exploring what works in a given context. This was, in fact, very much the approach I had been taking in my consulting work, but I had not yet made the direct connection to my research.

Until this point, I had assumed that the goal of my research was to come up with some universal type of formula for leadership transformation, even though finding such a formula was at odds with my beliefs and actual practice. But with Kets de Vries's words ringing in my ears, I realized that leadership transformation was something that could only ever be understood holistically — through the subtleties, nuances, and idiosyncrasies of the "protagonists" involved. So Richard, Skye, and I chose to go down a very different path from the formula-driven texts that we all found so frustrating. It proved liberating.

Our original research centered on seven leaders of CEO status from my management consulting practice. Their success in transforming themselves, their leadership teams, and their organizations had been well documented. They had seen radical improvement in 360-degree feedback on their personal effectiveness and the effectiveness of their teams, along with significant gains for their organizations in measures like financial performance, customer approval, and employee engagement.

Based on my level of intimacy and trust with each of these leaders — developed over many years of working closely together through good times and bad — I sought to develop a rich and contextual understanding of leadership transformation through their eyes. Their humility and their willingness to be vulnerable was paramount to the findings, with each leader giving me license to tell the "warts and all" version of the story.

We captured these stories through a series of lengthy interviews, conducted a rigorous linguistic analysis, and discovered several themes common to all in the challenges they had faced and the strategies they had used to meet those challenges.

In subsequent conversations, and inspired by Karl Weick's assertion that "people see more things than they can describe in words," we found that the best way to elicit a deep and broad discussion of those key themes and to describe the leaders' mastery of what they had learned was through the use of metaphor.

Ultimately we uncovered seven distinct yet interdependent metaphors that resonated powerfully with the participants: Fire (ambition), Snowball (accountability and momentum), Master Chef (frameworks, tools, and strategies), Coach (support and feedback), Mask (authenticity), Movie (self-reflection), and Russian Dolls (coordinating multiple journeys).

These may sound familiar or even trite, but each contains deep and powerful insights into how leaders can become more effective. The familiarity of the words makes them memorable — helpful when trying to change entrenched behavior — and easier to discuss with a group. What's more, the seven metaphors are designed to be generative in nature. Unlike lists, steps, and formulas, which are rigid and don't allow for interpretation and personalization, the nature of metaphors is that they can be unfolded. They allow us to open up our thinking, inspire our creativity, and help us discover complementary and related meanings and applications.

Over the last three years, my colleagues and I have shared these stories and applied these metaphors in consulting, speaking, and teaching engagements to thousands of leaders on four continents. They have proven to be reliable catalysts for purposeful reflection and meaningful action.

More important, they have allowed us to dramatically accelerate the process of leadership transformation in our clients, and thus greatly widened the data pool for this book. We now have hundreds of compelling stories of leadership transformation to draw upon — at the CEO and the executive level — many of which you will read about in this book.

One thing you may notice is that all of the stories in this book are each a little different. That's because there is no one way, no cookie-cutter program by which to apply the seven metaphors. They only make sense in the unique context of each leader's journey.

So *Leadership Transformed* is not just about leaders who have transformed themselves and their organizations. It's about transforming the way we think about leadership: to one where the art is as important as the science.

Quantifying transformation

For those of you who like science, fear not; the leadership transformations we documented in our research were not just anecdotal. Quantitative data on these shifts were captured by the 360-degree survey instrument we used with our leaders — Leadership/Impact (a registered trademark of Human Synergistics International), developed by Dr. Robert Cooke, associate professor emeritus of Managerial Studies at the University of Illinois at Chicago and CEO of Human Synergistics International. For more information on this tool, why I rate it so highly, and how to access it, please go to the appendix at the back of this book.

It won't surprise you to learn that nearly all leaders aspire to make a constructive impact on others. Visually, this is represented in the Leadership/Impact graph by the predominance of the color blue (dark gray) and the absence of the colors red (mid gray), denoting an aggressive-defensive impact, and green (light gray), denoting a passive-defensive impact — see figure 1a.

It also won't surprise you to learn that there is usually a substantial gap between the impact a leader would like to be making and the impact actually being made in the eyes of that leader's stakeholders — see the marked difference between figures 1a and 1b. This was also the case for the CEOs in my original doctoral research.

Leadership/Impact® ANZ Averages (2010)

Ideal Impact (described by Self)
n=5673 Leaders

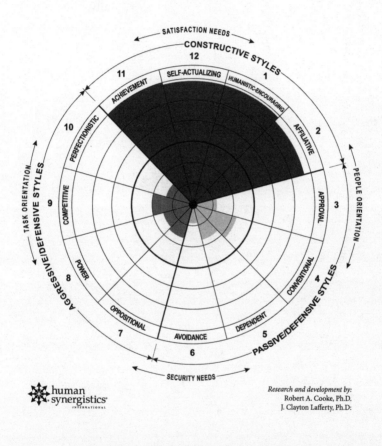

Copyright © 1973-2013 by Human Synergistics International. All rights reserved.

Figure 1a

Leadership/Impact® ANZ Averages (2010)

Actual Impact (described by 41,408 Others)
n=5673 Leaders

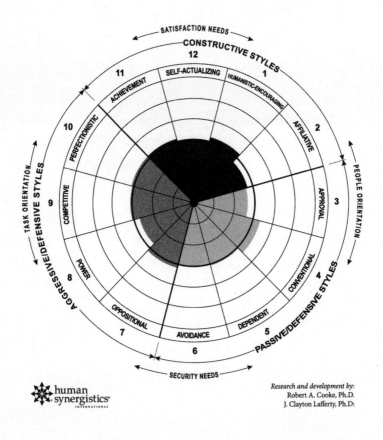

Copyright © 1973-2013 by Human Synergistics International. All rights reserved.

Figure 1b

Figure 2a shows the aggregate actual impact of the original CEOs at the outset of their journeys, which is even less constructive than the average of all leaders in a database of more than forty thousand executives.

Over time, the original CEOs were able to dramatically shift their actual impact, as can be seen in figure 2b. This most recent measure places our subjects among the top 10 percent of Constructive profiles within the database. It was this shift that provided us with undeniable evidence of leadership transformation. It also provided us with an academically credible departure point for what then became a highly qualitative study: to uncover the central themes behind such a shift.

Notwithstanding the importance of this data, I want to stress that my definition of transformation is informed by, but not limited to, the Leadership/Impact tool. In the original research, and indeed for this book, I selected leaders who also demonstrated evidence of transformation in their executive teams and in the performance of their organizations on such critical measures as financial results, customer advocacy, and employee engagement. Most important, I selected leaders who would truly provide an honest and authentic account of their journeys rather than perpetuate the flawed "heroic" notions of leadership that sent me on this journey in the first place. I am forever indebted to the leaders in this book for their trust, honesty, and vulnerability in allowing me to tell their stories authentically.

Leadership/Impact®
The Actual Impact of Our Research CEOS

First Measure (described by 46 Others)
n=7 Leaders

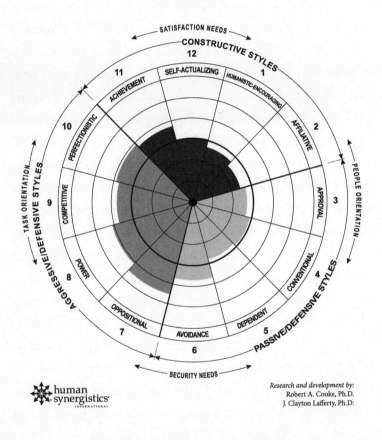

Research and development by:
Robert A. Cooke, Ph.D.
J. Clayton Lafferty, Ph.D.

Figure 2a

Copyright © 1973-2013 by Human Synergistics International. All rights reserved.

Leadership/Impact®
The Actual Impact of Our Research CEOS

Final Measure (described by 50 Others)
n=7 Leaders

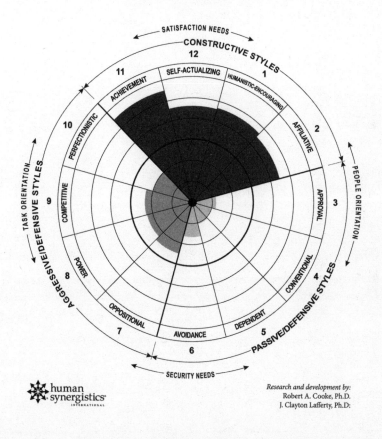

Research and development by:
Robert A. Cooke, Ph.D.
J. Clayton Lafferty, Ph.D.

Copyright © 1973-2013 by Human Synergistics International. All rights reserved.

Figure 2b

Introduction

I N T H E B O O K ' S S E V E N main chapters, each of the seven metaphors for leadership transformation will be explored in detail. The seven metaphors are represented visually in figure 3.

The 7 Metaphors for Leadership Transformation®

Research and Development by Dr. Peter Fuda. ©2010. All Rights Reserved

Figure 3

In the Fire chapter, we'll look at the motivational forces that initiate and sustain transformation efforts. In a departure from conventional change literature, I'll move beyond the notion of a "burning platform" — an idea coined by consultant Daryl Conner in the late 1980s and popularized thereafter by Professor John Kotter to denote urgency and commitment to change — to the notion of a "burning ambition." In this critical shift, I outline how to move from a mindset of perennial fear and urgency to a far more energizing context that provides the fuel to sustain what is often a long and arduous journey of transformation. In addition, we'll explore the distinction between organizational versus personal imperatives for change. I'll present a four-quadrant matrix that allows you to plot your motivation across each of these dimensions and assess your level of "fuel for the fire."

The Snowball chapter explores the notion of accountability, and the consequent momentum or "snowball effect" that occurs when a critical mass of leaders commits to principles of constructive leadership. I'll break down several aspects of the metaphor, including how to make the Snowball roll faster, sweeping more leaders into the process, and how to eliminate the friction generated by leaders who aren't committed to the journey. Finally, we'll look at how to create a tightly compacted Snowball by embedding the principles of constructive leadership into organizational systems and structures. At this point, the Snowball becomes an almost unstoppable force with the potential to crash through all obstacles.

In the Master Chef chapter, we'll take a look at how to "artfully" apply leadership frameworks, tools, and strategies throughout a transformation effort. I liken the change frameworks to a chef's recipes, the leadership tools and diagnostics to a chef's utensils, and the various leadership strategies to a chef's cooking techniques. I then discuss how, on their own, none of these elements are remarkable; the majority of transformation efforts fail despite the presence of all of these ingredients. Having the frameworks, tools, and strategies is not enough; in fact, they can give us a false sense of security. It is their artful application that can make the difference between success and failure. The metaphor grants deep insights into how a leader can progress thoughtfully from amateur cook to master chef — the latter being able to deploy frameworks, tools, and strategies in highly contextual and creative ways.

In the Coach chapter, I use a sports analogy to distinguish between several important roles in the leadership coaching process. The leader is captain of the team, a role clearly different from that of the coach. Unlike the traditional notion, I position coaching as most effective when it comes from a range of stakeholders, including the formal coaching staff (consultants), teammates (the leader's team and colleagues on the journey with them), and fans (the leader's family and personal relationships). I address the fundamental issues of creating trust among the different stakeholder groups and an environment where each has a mutual stake in the outcome of the coaching.

The fifth chapter will draw upon two examples from popular culture to explore the various Masks a leader can wear and the impact of those Masks. The first is the mask of the Broadway musical *Phantom of the Opera*, whose function is to conceal imperfections. The second is the 1994 Jim Carrey film *The Mask*, which concerns adopting a persona that isn't aligned with one's authentic self, values, or aspirations. In both cases, the Mask produces adverse effects on both the leader and those he or she leads. We'll explore how leaders can shed the heavy burden of wearing a Mask in favor of a more congruent "best self" that draws on their unique purpose, strengths, and values.

In the sixth chapter, we'll investigate three different aspects of the Movie metaphor to explore how leaders can develop critical capabilities of self-awareness and reflection. The first aspect is the notion of being trapped in a repeating scenario, as in the Bill Murray classic *Groundhog Day*. The second aspect is the editing suite — equivalent to leaders reflecting on their actions after key interactions. Once proficiency has been reached in the editing suite, the final aspect of the metaphor is becoming the director of one's own Movie: a leader able to take control and direct a new Movie with a story line that is in keeping with his or her vision. We'll also look at techniques that allow leaders to slow down their Movies and choose a better course of action in real time.

The concluding chapter, Russian Dolls, will explore the various journeys interconnected with a leader's own journey of transformation, which I represent as dolls-within-dolls. These may include, but are not limited to, a personal doll, a leadership doll, a team doll, an organizational doll, and an up-line doll. I use the notion of "up-line" to represent the hierarchy above the leader; this might be an international parent company, a board of directors, or a state or federal regulatory body. Within the metaphor of the Russian Dolls, this constitutes the largest or outermost doll. We'll investigate the notion of doll (stakeholder) management, on the premise that when the dolls fit neatly within one another, they have the potential to travel well together. I'll pay particular attention to managing expectations of the up-line doll, such as the corporate parent or board of directors, which has the potential to "swallow" all of the other dolls — and the leadership agenda along with it.

How the book is going to work

Each of the seven main chapters will provide an in-depth explanation of the respective metaphor, its individual parts, and how it may be best used to enhance your leadership effectiveness. The metaphors each promote meaningful reflection and purposeful action in a different way. Each chapter will be filled with stories and anecdotes from the original subjects of my doctoral research, as well as from many other leaders who have since used the metaphors to accelerate their journeys.

While I discuss the seven metaphors in seven separate chapters — a somewhat unnatural but necessary convention — you will pretty quickly get a sense of the relationships between them. This is one reason why most of the leaders in this book appear in multiple chapters; it was all but impossible to limit their stories to one metaphor, and it would have been inauthentic to try.

Moving beyond inspiration to purposeful action

I have been personally inspired by the leaders in this book on my own journey as a business leader, consultant, and researcher, and I hope you will be too. But my wish is for you to go beyond inspiration, and to successfully apply these lessons yourself. To help you do this, my colleagues and I have designed a very comprehensive set of free resources on my blog. These resources include sophisticated audiovisual material such as three-minute animations of each metaphor and documentary-style footage of many of the leaders in the book. They also include dozens of exercises that will allow you to put the metaphors into practice on your own or with your team. Until now, these resources have only been available to the clients of our management consultancy, so I'm excited to share them with you. To access these resources, simply go to my blog, www.peterfuda.com, and follow the prompts.

If you're action oriented, you might like to visit the website at the end of each chapter to complete the exercises and interact with the audiovisual resources. If you're more reflective, then consider reading the whole book first, before visiting the website. Either way, the book and website have been designed so that you can choose your own adventure — so have fun!

1

Fire

The Fire metaphor describes the motivational forces that initiate and sustain transformation efforts, including a burning platform and a burning ambition, as well as personal and organizational reasons for change.

Fire is, of course, an often-used concept to describe motivation, with heat representing emotional intensity in various forms such as anger, passion, love, urgency, and desire. It was the two applications of "urgency" and "desire" that granted us our first significant insights into the phenomenon of leadership transformation. In a business context, the metaphor of fire has typically been used to denote urgency. Yet when we looked deeply into our cases of transformation, this was not all that we found.

Consider Tim's story. At just thirty-three, without a university degree, he had still risen to managing director of an iconic advertising agency — it was like something out of a fairy tale. In our first interaction, he sported the swagger of a confident young executive rapidly scaling the heights of his industry, someone who was headhunted into one of the biggest advertising jobs in the country. I was simultaneously energized and overwhelmed by Tim's passion and enthusiasm. Yet his confidence was undermined somewhat by a slight shortness of breath; something I attributed to his being heavy for his size. There were additional signs that all was not as it seemed: when Tim spoke, he would struggle to hold prolonged eye contact, and he kept referencing impressive elements of his past as though he were pitching himself to a prospective client.

After a few short months in the role, Tim's fairy tale began to unravel. His new organization lost several important clients, and with them, much of its historical luster. It needed a big shift in commercial performance, and a revitalization of its creative reputation; all of this against the background of an impending sale to a multinational. Under enormous pressure and scrutiny, it soon became apparent to Tim that he might have reached the limits of his natural toolset. His charisma, street smarts, and creative flair had expedited his trip up the corporate ladder, but they were no longer compensating for his lack of leadership maturity.

Tim developed a story in his mind that he was a victim of his superiors' "erratic behavior" and limited leadership skills. He felt they were placing unreasonable demands on him and he resented their expectations. These negative sentiments soon developed into full-blown paranoia: Tim became convinced that they were plotting to remove him from his role and from the organization altogether.

Despite the story Tim was telling himself under pressure, in lucid moments he reflected on his own failings and even suggested that he might be perpetuating the very same issues he was having difficulty handling. In one conversation, Tim told me that he was experiencing "professional schizophrenia," fluctuating between strong self-confidence and no confidence at all, between high motivation and complete disinterest. On reflection, his personal appearance matched his chaotic demeanor: heavy, sluggish, and disheveled.

The turning point in Tim's journey came when he reconnected with his inner fire in the form of a personal statement of purpose and aspiration. Tim felt that, since accepting the leadership role, he had been consumed by burning platforms, so, for contrast, we labeled this statement his personal burning ambition (figure 4).

Greater clarity of purpose motivated Tim to raise his standards both professionally and personally. He embraced yoga, shed a significant amount of weight, and revitalized spiritual practices that helped him to stay calm and centered. He openly addressed the poor impact he was having on his team, and in-

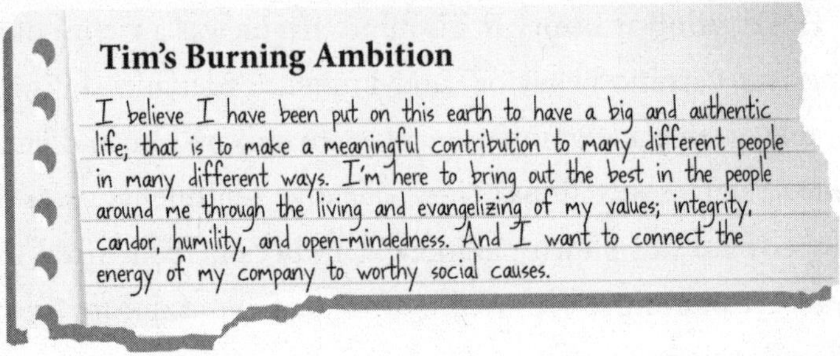

> **Tim's Burning Ambition**
>
> I believe I have been put on this earth to have a big and authentic life; that is to make a meaningful contribution to many different people in many different ways. I'm here to bring out the best in the people around me through the living and evangelizing of my values; integrity, candor, humility, and open-mindedness. And I want to connect the energy of my company to worthy social causes.

Figure 4

vited them to help him change. He let go of the victim mindset and made a concerted effort to establish productive relationships with his superiors. In the subsequent months, he successfully led his organization through a tumultuous period in its history; employee commitment, customer satisfaction, and financial performance all rose.

Following the sale of his company, Tim accepted an even bigger job as the CEO of a rival agency. Empowered by his new insights, Tim translated his personal burning ambition for "a big and authentic life" into an ambition for his new organization. In early 2007, Tim became one of three founding directors on a new initiative called Earth Hour. The goal of this initiative was to raise awareness of climate change by getting the residents of Sydney, Australia, to simultaneously turn off their lights for one hour. In order to achieve this outcome, Tim had to engage and influence a very disparate group of stakeholders including the media, big business, politicians, and the general public.

In the end, a staggering 2.5 million Sydneysiders participated in the event, including the prime minister. The lights were even turned off in the Sydney Opera House and on the Harbour Bridge! In recognition of this extraordinary result, Tim's advertising agency was awarded the Titanium Award, considered the most prestigious advertising award in the world, at the 2007 Cannes Advertising Awards. In the years since Tim helped found Earth Hour, its momentum as a social change initiative has escalated beyond his wildest dreams. In 2012, 6,950 cities from 152 countries participated in this symbolic fight against climate change, affecting billions of people worldwide.

Tim's story is an impressive illustration of a leader's motivational fire shifting over time, and the positive outcomes associated with such a shift. But why are we talking about motivation if this is a book about *how* leaders transform? I confess that the Fire metaphor was something I stumbled on quite by accident, and initially even I questioned its validity as a theme for transformation. Thanks to Tim and the many other leaders in this book, I now understand how central Fire is to all of the other metaphors, and to how leaders actually transform.

Before addressing how my subjects had made such substantial shifts in their personal, team, and organizational effectiveness, I asked them *why* they had committed to a journey of transformation in the first place. Originally, I asked why to understand the context in which the changes took place. Having worked closely with each leader along the journey, I felt this question would give me a bit of colorful context for each leader's story. Having witnessed many of their struggles, I was also keen to get on the record what it is that possesses a leader to invest the time, money, and energy that are always required in an undertaking of this nature. But while the context I got was indeed colorful, I soon came to understand that the leaders' motivations revealed far more significant insights about change than I had imagined.

Tim's story illustrates something of a dance around four quadrants of motivation, which are illustrated in the Fire Matrix (figure 5). The four quadrants are formed by two axes, the first of which is the burning platform versus burning ambition axis.

It was management consultant Daryl Conner who first

The Fire Matrix©

ORGANIZATIONAL

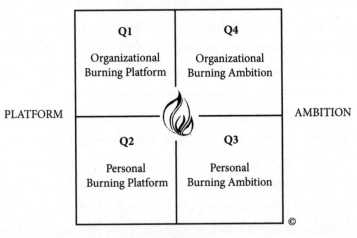

Research and Development by Dr. Peter Fuda. ©2010. All Rights Reserved

Figure 5

coined the concept of the burning platform, and Harvard professor John Kotter who popularized the idea as the critical prerequisite for successful change efforts. It derives from a real-life tragedy that occurred on July 6, 1988, on the Piper Alpha oil platform in the North Sea, when 167 men lost their lives.

One of the survivors of the catastrophe was Andy Mochan, a superintendent on the rig. Woken by a huge explosion, he ran up on deck to discover that the platform was engulfed in flames. He faced a choice: Stay on the platform and burn to death, or jump some hundred and fifty feet — approximately fifteen stories — into freezing cold water and hope to survive? He decided to jump. Somehow he survived the impact and was picked up by a rescue boat just before he would have frozen to death. When asked why he jumped, he replied, "Better probable death than certain death."

The apparent application of this story to a business context is that fear and urgency are not only necessary but desirable motivators for change. As Kotter explains in his book, *Leading Change*, "Visible crises can be enormously helpful in catching people's attention and pushing up urgency levels. Conducting business as usual is very difficult if the building seems to be on fire."

But while a burning platform can spark leaders into action, what we found strongly suggests that a mindset of urgency and fear is not conducive to sustaining change over time. Our findings also suggest that in a world of burning platforms, there are many pyromaniacs. As Kotter himself seems to agree, fires can cause collateral damage if not tended to. Our work leads us to conclude that it is, in fact, a burning ambition — a strong desire-driven motivation — that enables leaders to accelerate and sustain transformation efforts over time.

Beyond the burning platform/burning ambition dichotomy, there is an additional nuance to the Fire metaphor that became starkly evident in our research: a leader's motivation is most powerful when it encompasses both organizational and individual imperatives for change. The Fire Matrix enables us to explore the effects of these motivational forces on a leader's ability to transform. Let's take a closer look at the four quadrants.

Quadrant 1: Organizational Burning Platform

Consistent with Kotter, we found that leaders are readily able to list the problems and issues that have motivated them to undertake a transformation effort. Time after time, we would hear statements like "Our financial trajectory is poor," "Our competitors are more aggressive," "Our customers are squeezing us," or "Our staff engagement is at an all-time low."

Over the last couple of years, I have discussed this quadrant with large numbers of executives all around the world. As a result of these discussions, I have come to understand the pervasiveness of the burning platform: leaders often operate from the belief that nothing significant happens without a crisis. Leaders also need to justify large investments of time, money, and resources to their stakeholders when undertaking a transformation effort, and an organizational burning platform seems to provide a compelling way to do just that.

A case in point is Alan, who when I first met him had just been appointed the new CEO of a German chemical and pharmaceutical multinational subsidiary. Alan was casually dressed in slacks and an open-neck shirt, at odds with the formality I had experienced at reception a few minutes earlier. He looked like the pictures I had seen of the dashing race-car drivers of the fifties: a handsome middle-aged British gentleman showing just the right amount of wear and tear.

He painted a very colorful picture of the organization he had inherited; he called it a "Prussian empire" where pulling rank and bullying were acceptable behaviors. He reeled off stories about the "rottweilers" in reception who made guests feel unwelcome, and parking-lot antics where staff fearfully moved their cars if the boss parked next to them so that he wouldn't know what time they went home. His new staff quaked when he walked the floor because a previous CEO had placed photographs of messy desks in reception with the message "If this desk is yours, come and see me in my office." Legend had it that offenders were never seen again.

Not surprisingly, a Hewitt Employee Engagement survey undertaken by Alan's outgoing predecessor placed the organization in the bottom 10 percent of all employers in the country. In addition, a damning management audit revealed that only 30 percent of staff trusted their leaders. As if this was not enough of a burning platform for change, profits and revenue had been flat for several years, and because of an aging population there were limited options for natural growth.

Given the highly centralized nature of his organization, Alan knew that he had limited control over levers such as strategy and structure. In our early conversations, the notion that "leadership creates culture and culture drives performance" really resonated with him. He adopted this as his mantra and touted it to anyone who would listen, as well as to those who wouldn't.

Alan's case for organizational change was as compelling as any that I had heard. Yet as with every leader I have worked with, there turned out to be more to it than met the eye. Despite distancing himself from the "appalling" behavior of his predecessors and international colleagues, it turned out that Alan had in fact internalized their power-centric antics, and was himself displaying many of the behaviors he professed to despise, such as encouraging his staff to compete with one another for his attention. Alan later revealed to me that he had been desperate to embark on a *personal* journey of transformation, and it just so happened that I had been in the right place, at the right time, with the right message.

Quadrant 2: Personal Burning Platform

When I partner with leaders on their quest for more effective leadership, they gradually begin to open up about their personal fears, challenges, and insecurities, represented by the second quadrant of the matrix. For example, they say things such as "My reputation is on the line—I'll look really stupid if I can't build a company of substance," or "Every day I try out a different approach, but nothing seems to work," or "I'm physically exhausted; I can't keep going like this."

The story of Mike is a case in point. He had just become the CEO of a large U.S. multinational subsidiary specializing in IT outsourcing. Mike's dream, ever since he was a boy, had been to ascend to the top job; he'd wanted to follow in the footsteps of his father, the CEO and chairman of a large British manufacturing company.

Like Alan, Mike had inherited an organizational burning platform, but I sensed that his desire to engage in transformation was also very personal. I have a vivid recollection of our first meeting in the spring of 2003. After I was ushered into his office, I shook hands with a man of average height and build with brown hair and a heavy Canadian accent. His distinguishing feature was a thick moustache like the one my dad wore in the seventies before my siblings and I made him shave it off. Mike didn't smile when he shook my hand or hold eye contact for very long. Most CEOs I had met up to that point radiated some kind of presence. Mike just looked lost.

Mike could recite a long list of reasons as to why his company needed a comprehensive change process. The big deals were drying up, his competitors were strengthening, customers were becoming increasingly sophisticated, employees were disengaged after years of cost-cutting, his executive team was dysfunctional, and so on. Later, Mike confirmed what we both knew instinctively in that first meeting: most of his motivation to engage was, in fact, personal. Having occupied leadership roles his whole life — from school prefect and captain of the hockey team to a sales manager leading a team of people twice his age — Mike had a multitude of trophies and trinkets to testify that he was the right man to lead the way out of the fire. But truth be told, his credentials didn't necessarily stretch far enough for him to cope with the top leadership role. He had gotten the job largely on the basis of his sharp financial skills and operational acumen; he would often boast that he could "spot a mistake in a spreadsheet from fifty yards." But he wasn't comfortable with customers and felt awkward around staff.

Mike's insecurities resulted in some very erratic leadership behavior during his first few months in the role, and his first informal appraisal with his new boss didn't go so well; his boss explained in very short syllables that "we have gotten off to a very bad start." Mike tried the usual quick-fix strategies, such as the two-day "team building" offsite, but nothing worked. Deep down, Mike knew that the only way he could transform his organization was to start by transforming his own leadership — so the personal burning platform became very clear.

In the years since, I have learned that the personal motivation for change is often concealed beneath more obvious organizational forces. In an attempt to live up to pervasive notions of the "heroic leader" and avoid looking weak, senior executives will bury or otherwise disguise their personal motivations for engaging in a transformation effort. This was certainly the case with Mike, and it slowed his journey in the early stages. Only after his personal imperative for change became quite public, as he engaged his colleagues in the changes he was seeking to make, did Mike's leadership transformation accelerate. In the five years that followed, he not only dramatically shifted his personal effectiveness, he led his organization to almost double its revenue and more than triple its profits.

In the earlier stages of my consulting career, I didn't probe deeply into a leader's personal fears and concerns, partly because they didn't offer them up easily, partly because I didn't want to risk losing the consulting engagement, and partly because I suspected they would emerge over time as we built trust in the relationship — which is what usually did happen. What I now understand is that respectfully probing into a leader's personal fears from the very first interaction is actually one of the fastest ways to build trust in the relationship. Perhaps more important, it allows leaders to quickly shift away from hiding what they fear most and toward realizing their deepest personal ambitions.

Quadrant 3: Personal Burning Ambition

It is in the third quadrant of the Fire Matrix, the personal burning ambition, that I have found that a leader's commitment and personal accountability for change really begin to accelerate. Quadrants 1 and 2 are about running from a fire; quadrant 3 describes a fire that burns inside. As Stephen R. Covey once said, "Motivation is a fire from within. If someone else tries to light that fire under you, chances are it will burn very briefly."

The motivation behind a personal burning ambition is evident in statements like "I want to live a big and authentic life," "I want to increase my health and happiness," "I want to align my work with a strong sense of purpose and meaning," or "I want to fulfill my leadership potential."

When leaders shift their focus away from what they want to avoid toward what they want to achieve, they experience a dramatic shift in energy—away from insecurity and perennial urgency and toward a calmer and more purposeful disposition. This in turn makes it possible to apply a more deliberate and disciplined effort toward realizing those ambitions.

Consider Dennis, the CEO of a division of a stock-exchange-listed insurance conglomerate. The conglomerate was only two years old, but the board wanted to grab a large share of the rapidly growing life insurance market, and they charged Dennis and his new division to go and get it.

Known as something of a legend in the industry, where he had had a long and distinguished actuarial career, Dennis had a reputation that preceded him. It was said of Dennis's intellect that he could tell you the answer before you asked the question. Even so, Dennis was a risky choice for the venture. Despite his impressive career, his track record was in fixing organizations, not growing them. And his first few months were shaky: Together with his team, Dennis had launched a go-to-market strategy with a lot of fanfare but little substance behind it, and as a result they were struggling with its execution. The board was demanding results, but his old approach wasn't working.

His executive team members were engaged in turf battles, and his broader staff lacked direction.

Before meeting Dennis, I had been warned that he could be intimidating both in stature and intellect. And indeed, six feet tall and broad-shouldered, Dennis looked quite fit for a man in his late fifties. When I met him for the first time, he cut an impressive figure in dark suit, striped silk tie, and designer glasses. But the thing that struck me most about him was the great big smile bursting out from behind his thick moustache.

I soon found that Dennis's big smile and intellectual horsepower hid a substantial personal burning platform. This was to be his last big job before retiring from management. His reputation and legacy were on the line, and things had been going poorly from the very beginning. This resulted in some erratic behavior. There were times during meetings when he would speak with the thoughtful sophistication of a Rhodes scholar, and others when he would convincingly impersonate the diction of a barroom brawler. For the first few months of our work together, it was two steps forward, three steps back.

It was only after we began to discuss Dennis's personal burning ambition that his trajectory became more positive and consistent. Dennis had a very strong desire to actually grow a business, not just fix a struggling one, before retiring. It was the very reason he had accepted the role in the first place, but amid the pressures of his first few months, he had lost sight of that and become fearful and anxious. It was as though his ambition to grow had slowly been overtaken by the desire to not fail.

This realization encouraged Dennis to make a very public disclosure to his team about his personal leadership vision. In a very powerful executive team meeting that is still etched in my mind today, he told them that what he wanted more than anything before he retired was to grow the organization. He wanted to unlock the potential of this budding new business and repay the board's faith in him. Most important, he wanted to leave a legacy for his people that they could build on in the years beyond his tenure. Dennis's team was blown away by his openness and trust in them, which energized him even further.

His renewed sense of personal ambition gave him clarity on the type of impact he would need to have on his team and organization in order to achieve his ambition. Rather than provide the answers, he would need to coach others to find their own solutions. Rather than show he was the smartest guy in the room, he would need to encourage others to express their ideas and challenge his. And rather than encourage his team to compete with one another, he would need to encourage them to collaborate.

Dennis really opened my eyes to the power of the personal burning ambition. As our relationship deepened, he shared an even broader vision with me. His ambition went beyond the scope of his work to his family life; he wanted to be a better father and husband. Dennis had had a tough upbringing, working in the local fruit markets from a very young age. His father's gambling and drinking habits devastated the family, one consequence being that Dennis had to keep paying off student loans long after he got his first job. This had a profound impact on Dennis, and he became very clear about his number one value, integrity. For him, that meant doing what you say you will, at all costs.

Fulfilling his personal ambition became the key focus for Dennis, and he embraced our work together with a renewed sense of vigor and determination. He asked that our monthly coaching sessions become fortnightly sessions. Every month, he was the first member of the executive team to update and circulate his personal action plan. He openly sought advice from peers who exemplified the leadership qualities he aspired to. And he put clear boundaries around his personal life to make sure he delivered at home as well as at work.

Over the following two years, Dennis measurably transformed his effectiveness as a leader, along with the effectiveness of his executive team. Employee engagement scores reached 80 percent, placing the company well above industry norms, and operating profit increased by 21 percent. Dennis entered retirement at age sixty with the sense of accomplishment and satisfaction that comes from having realized a personal ambition.

In Dennis's story and in many others, I have found that burning ambitions provide far greater leverage than burning platforms to keep leaders on track. All of the "transformed" leaders I have worked with faced days when it just felt too hard, where they encountered opposition, or where they were consumed by short-term pressures that demanded immediate attention. Clarity of personal ambition allows leaders to reorient their focus in spite of these competing pressures, and allows them to accept short-term pain in the pursuit of longer-term gain. Dennis's story also touches on the fourth and final quadrant of the matrix: Organizational Burning Ambition.

Quadrant 4: Organizational Burning Ambition

Leaders' personal ambitions are transcended by the lasting impact they wish to have on their organizations, their customers, their industries, and their communities. Leaders saying things like "I want to leave a legacy of a growing organization," "I want my successor to be set up for even greater success," "I want to transform our industry," "I want to revolutionize the customer experience," or "I want our organization to go beyond financial performance to societal contribution" are all expressions of the motivational forces at play in this quadrant.

Daniel H. Pink, author of *Drive: The Surprising Truth About What Motivates Us*, speaks about the power of purpose when it transcends the individual: "Autonomous people working toward mastery perform at very high levels. But those who do so in the service of some greater objective can achieve even more. The most deeply motivated people — not to mention the most productive and satisfied — hitch their desires to a cause larger than themselves."

We saw this play out on a grand scale with Tim connecting his desire for "a big and authentic life" to Earth Hour, one of the biggest social movements in recent times. But the shift from personal burning ambition to organizational burning ambition need not occur on such a grand scale to be powerful.

Christine was the highly articulate and ambitious CEO of a credit reporting and debt collection company — a very macho industry. When I started working with her in February 2005, she clearly had a burning platform to deal with: the company had been acquired by a private-equity firm and, in order to justify their investment, Christine had agreed on a plan with them to dramatically increase the financial performance of the business. She had put her own credibility on the line, but was not sure that her young team was up for the challenge. She had secured tens of millions of dollars in funding from some serious bankers and now it was all on her head. Privately, she wondered whether *she* was up for the challenge.

In the early days of the transformation effort, Christine responded to these massive pressures by tightening control, leaving nothing to chance, and demonstrating a tough, take-no-prisoners style of management. The result was enormous personal stress and a leadership team that was paralyzed; they depended on Christine for all important decisions and took none of the risks required to close the gap.

The shift in performance only started to happen when Christine connected with her deeply held desire to lead a significant transformation. She wanted to paint a picture of the possibilities that she saw, to help her team unlock their individual and collective potential and enable them to reach standards of performance that none of them thought possible. She knew that the only way to do this was to transform her impact on her organization and become the type of leader who brought out the best in others.

Christine wanted to break the monopoly that had existed for decades in the credit reporting market by creating another top-tier consumer bureau, which was something most experts thought was impossible. She wanted to provide consumers with greater choice and a much higher level of service than was the industry norm. And she succeeded: Over a period of five years, Christine transformed her leadership, her team, and her organization. Together, they increased revenue tenfold, broke the monopoly many considered unbreakable, and her company is now acknowledged as the industry benchmark.

My core insights from the Fire metaphor are threefold. First, shifting from a burning platform to a burning ambition is critical. While fear may provide the initial spark for action, aspiration is a far more important motivator. Sustainable change requires the fire of a burning ambition.

Second, it is vital for a leader to articulate not only the organizational reasons for change, but to delve deeper and establish very compelling personal motivations for change.

Finally, the Fire, or the *why*, is an integral part of *how* leaders transform. As Friedrich Nietzsche famously said, "He who has a why to live can bear almost any how." This is why I place Fire at the center of the seven metaphors — if the flame goes out, all other factors become redundant.

Now what?

If you're action oriented or itching to uncover your Fire, then I suggest you go to www.peterfuda.com and interact with the Fire audiovisual tools and exercises before coming back to read the next chapter. If you would prefer to keep reading, or you're not ready for any deep reflection yet, then here are a couple of simple next steps:

- Consider the extent to which you are motivated by a burning platform versus a burning ambition.
- Reflect on the forces compelling you to change personally.
- Add some "fuel to your fire" by reflecting on what you really want personally and professionally.

2

Snowball

The metaphor of the Snowball describes a virtuous cycle of accountability that propels the change effort forward. It starts with the leader, and builds momentum as others are swept up in the journey.

MY SECOND METAPHOR is the Snowball. Remember the Road Runner cartoons featuring Wile E. Coyote being swept up in a snowball as he careens down a snow-covered mountain? That image might make you wonder what this metaphor could possibly have to do with leadership transformation. But the truth is we can use it to describe a positive process through which something small and potentially insignificant builds upon itself over time, thereby becoming large, powerful, and eventually unstoppable.

Clynton was the managing director of a major multinational skin-care and beauty company headquartered in Germany. Over nine years, he had worked his way up from a junior marketing role until, at the tender age of thirty-four, he became the global corporation's youngest ever country manager. And wearing sleek designer suits and radiating genuine confidence and warmth, he looked the part. When I first met him, some three years after he had assumed the role, I thought he looked exactly the way the managing director of a skin-care company should — glowing, smooth, and polished.

Despite his youth and relative lack of leadership experience (compared to his counterparts in other countries), Clynton's division had enjoyed strong performance during his first three years in charge. In my conversations with him, however, I soon discovered that this level of performance was maintained at great personal cost. He put on a brave face, but was physically and mentally exhausted. Inside his organization, he was regarded as "Mr. Skincare" not only because of his extensive knowledge of all key aspects of the business, but also, and especially, because of his tendency to try to solve everyone's problems. To underline the point, he later said to me, "I thought I was being really efficient by finishing people's sentences!" Clynton had inadvertently instilled a sense of dependency in his team; they had come to rely on him for all important decisions, and also for the not-so-important ones.

Clynton faced ever-increasing growth demands from his parent company while powerful retailers pressured him to lower his wholesale prices. Rather than engage his team for support, Clynton continued to try to do it all himself. Eventually, though, something had to give, as he explained to me: "I was personally exhausted. I had been 'Mr. Skincare' for nine solid years and I just couldn't keep pushing the business by myself. I really needed to create an environment where my team could take the reins. It was probably a bit selfish; I wanted to get some space back and spend more time thinking about the future."

Clynton underwent a 360-degree feedback process along with his executive team in order to learn what kind of impact they were having on one another and their organization. When Clynton received his feedback, he was not surprised to find that his impact on his team was a long way from being ideal. Clynton's constant pushing of the business had created some very passive behaviors in the others. Everyone had learned to depend on him and to avoid making hard decisions themselves.

This feedback was a turning point for Clynton. He knew he had three options: hide the feedback, rationalize it away, or share it openly and honestly with the team. Clynton chose the third option, sharing his results and admitting for the very first time that he was tired and that he didn't have all the answers. But beyond sharing his pain, Clynton also shared his vision for the future, and asked his team for help leading the company toward it.

In the following weeks, Clynton opened up to the company at large at an annual leadership forum and shared his feedback and his intention to change with his top sixty leaders. He invited all of them to join him on a quest to become the best leaders they could be. By opening up in this way, Clynton was committing not only to make changes personally; he was very consciously setting a standard—and an agenda—for others to follow. This was the beginning of a snowball effect, as he later explained to me: "By engaging my executive team this way, I set up an expectation of the kind of leader I aspired to be. They hold me accountable to that. At the same time, I hold them accountable to the same standards. By engaging the second level of leaders, I've ensured that they will hold my executive team accountable, as I do from another direction. We now have three layers embedded in the process. And so it continues; it's like a massive snowball rolling down the hill, with me trapped in the middle."

As more leaders in Clynton's organization were swept up in the process, its momentum increased. Team members flourished as patterns of deferred decision making gave way to increased personal initiative. For example, divisional leaders took the lead in designing more efficient processes to remove costs and bureaucracy from the organization. They sourced better products less expensively from different countries around the globe. Collectively they advanced toward their vision faster and faster, resulting in each of their key brands reaching number one or number two status in their respective categories. Clynton's effectiveness as a leader surged. His organization has since gone on to outperform much larger competitors for six consecutive years—and counting.

It is worth noting that Clynton's comments about being

"trapped" in the Snowball, while tongue-in-cheek, do contain a serious undertone. Once the process was under way, there was no way he could waver from his stated intention without answering to all of the others who surrounded him in the Snowball. This "entrapment" applied to every other leader in the organization. Those who could not cope with the increased personal accountability and responsibility left, and new team members who thrived in this type of environment joined.

I have found that when an individual leader is simultaneously held accountable by his superiors *and* those who directly report to him, there is an exponential increase in momentum toward more effective leadership. And this effect is not reserved for the leader at the center of the Snowball. Let's take a look in more detail at how others are swept up in the process.

The view from below

Consider the Snowball metaphor from the perspective of one of Clynton's team members — his sales director, Bernie. By Bernie's own admission, nothing ever came easily to him. He grew up in a government housing project with parents who were violent toward each other and their kids; Bernie and his siblings were often left to fend for themselves. Not surprisingly, he developed a desire to live a very different kind of life. In the work environment, Bernie wore his high personal standards as a badge of honor. He had worked in big organizations all his life, and he felt very confident in his ability to manage people. He was also very protective of his sales team, and reacted badly to colleagues who tried to "interfere in his patch."

Bernie's private life, meanwhile, was nothing short of chaotic. He had moved cities with his wife and three-month-old baby to take up the role. But rather than embarking on an exciting new life in a new home with his family, Bernie found himself working twelve hours a day, day after day. Still, he felt that no matter how hard he worked, he could "never get on top of it all." He consoled himself with the belief that he was doing a good job for the organization and his sales team. Then he underwent the feedback process with Clynton, and this belief was shaken to the core.

Bernie learned that his peers found him dismissive, adversarial, and territorial. What concerned him most, however, was his impact on his subordinates. His very directive and dominating style had created high levels of dependency among his own team. So while he was working around the clock, they were struggling to have any kind of impact on the business.

Based on Bernie's self-image as a high achiever and an accomplished manager, there was a real danger of his becoming defensive and dismissing his feedback, but luckily he was swept up into the Snowball that was starting to roll from the top of the organization. First and foremost, Bernie found Clynton's humility inspiring and wanted to give his own team that same sense of inspiration. Never one to accept half measures, Bernie decided he wouldn't be happy with the baseline 10 percent improvement sought by Clynton's team. He wanted to take this opportunity to "revolutionize his leadership and his life."

Bernie shared his feedback with his own team one-on-one and collectively, and invited them to offer suggestions for how to improve his leadership. Their insights led him to make a whole range of changes quickly: instead of obsessing about how his team were doing their jobs, he focused primarily on results; instead of demanding long reports loaded with information, he asked for short summaries with clear recommendations; instead of demanding everything immediately, he learned to wait until the next day. He started going home at 5:30 P.M. and never again sent e-mails late at night.

Bernie also changed his attitude toward his peers: he scheduled regular, one-on-one meetings to get to know them as people, invited their opinions on how to boost sales, and initiated meetings between his team and theirs so that they could set joint goals.

Bernie's transformation was rapid and substantial. He was able to develop trusting relationships with colleagues, and his sales team made a huge contribution to the overall financial performance of the organization. Bernie is now widely regarded as a role model across his organization, but it is the changes in his personal life that gratify him most. Through the process, Bernie gained a new appreciation of his own value, and is now a mentor to many members of his extended family who are grappling with how to transform their own lives, whether in the professional or the personal realm.

Clynton and Bernie's stories help us make sense of the two dominant themes of the Snowball metaphor: accountability and momentum. The Snowball is a self-amplifying structure that feeds on itself; this process can manifest itself in a negative and a positive way, as a vicious or virtuous cycle. But alongside this cyclical motion, the Snowball follows a linear trajectory down a mountain, as represented in figure 6.

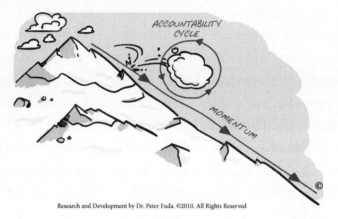

Research and Development by Dr. Peter Fuda. ©2010. All Rights Reserved

Figure 6

The cyclical motion of the metaphor allows us to explore the mutually reinforcing cycle of accountability that develops between leaders and their subordinates who engage in a leadership agenda. The trajectory down the mountain allows us to explore the sense of momentum toward stated leadership goals, which seems to result from this mutual accountability.

Motion I—A cycle of mutual accountability

For Clynton—and most of the other leaders you'll meet in these pages—there was a clear moment in their journeys when the

Snowball was well and truly set in motion. This point of no return came when they openly acknowledged their shortcomings and flaws, and made a public declaration to others regarding their desire to change.

Typically, the initial feedback process reveals a substantial gap between how a leader would like to be leading, and how that leader is actually experienced by others. Seeing this gap—which, in some instances, you could safely describe as a gaping abyss—requires real humility and a willingness to make yourself vulnerable, often to your subordinates. Yet despite many leaders' initial trepidation (or outright terror), this act of showing vulnerability is almost always perceived by their colleagues as a show of strength and courage, inspiring peers and subordinates to follow suit and mirror the leaders' public declaration and commitment to change.

My friend, the researcher and author Brené Brown, explains it like this in her book, *Daring Greatly: How the Courage to Be Vulnerable Transforms the Way We Love, Live, Parent, and Lead*: "Vulnerability sounds like truth and feels like courage. Truth and courage aren't always comfortable, but they're never weakness."

To illustrate this concept, I will now return to the story of Mike, whom we met in the Fire chapter. Six months after becoming CEO, Mike had initiated a 360-degree feedback process for himself and his entire executive team. The day arrived to receive the data and he found himself nervously sitting at the boardroom table along with his twelve direct reports. The results were going to be represented in the Leadership/Impact graph, so naturally Mike was hoping his own profile would be a "sea of blue" with little or no red or green, confirmation that he did indeed motivate and encourage people to achieve their goals and work effectively as a team. But as he opened up his folder, he saw a mass of red and green. Indeed, Mike had been motivating and encouraging his team — to compete among themselves, oppose one another's ideas, and avoid responsibility!

From the sheer volume of red and green staring him in the face, Mike suspected this might possibly represent the single worst feedback profile ever recorded. Even more worryingly, he was the CEO — the leader — and everyone else on the team was all but guaranteed to have better results than him. It was at that moment that I asked the group: "Who will be first to share their data with the team?" Mike was smart enough to know that this was a rhetorical question.

As he contemplated the "horror story" staring him in the face, Mike briefly considered "firing the bastards" (those would have been his team members in the room with him) who had given him such feedback. Instead, he swallowed his pride and followed through on a commitment he had made to me in an earlier discussion: that he would openly share his feedback with the team, no matter what it said.

As he slowly stood, I saw a red flush spread upward from Mike's shirt collar and progressively engulf his neck and face. Clearing his throat, he forced himself to make eye contact with his team. "We have a problem," he began. You could have cut the atmosphere with a knife. "I think the printer has run out of blue ink!" The ensuing silence was finally broken by nervous laughter. Encouraged, Mike took a breath and continued. "This is my profile, but this is not what I aspire to. I'm not happy with it, and I'm committed to change." He then looked at each one of his subordinates and asked them to hold him accountable to his vision for his leadership.

Mike has told me that this moment was one of the hardest of his entire career — but that he's very glad he handled it the way he did. His concern, like that of most leaders, was that exposing his failings would be perceived as a public display of weakness. He was surprised when, on the contrary, his team lauded him for showing real courage. For Mike, this was the moment his Snowball began to roll.

While Mike's "horrific" feedback is certainly an extreme example, most of the leaders I have worked with have faced similarly humbling moments when they attempt to be transparent about the nature of their challenges with their subordinates. In every case, that leader's humility and vulnerability became a key factor in the ultimate trajectory of their Snowball.

Leaders who are humble create a safer and more open environment for discussion and feedback regarding their impact, which can help them both collect and use good data quickly. When leaders declare their intention to change, their colleagues are more inclined to give them the benefit of the doubt as they make their first, often clumsy steps down this path. And leaders who invite open feedback are more likely to enlist a host of coaches among their colleagues to help them align their present impact with their leadership vision.

Most important, there is a consequence when leaders make a public commitment to change and invite others to hold them to account. As we saw in Clynton and Mike's stories, such a declaration creates an implicit expectation that team members will follow their lead and make a similar commitment. In effect, all members of a team become accountable to one another in their quest to become more effective leaders.

In this context, regardless of their position in the formal hierarchy, each team member has the power to call out behavior that is not aligned with the stated intention. Consequently, leaders create a Snowball of mutual accountability with themselves at the center and their team compacted around them, all aligned to the same desire for increased leadership effectiveness.

Practically speaking, leaders become implicitly accountable to people under their direct authority. In so doing, they flip the traditional hierarchy and yield their positional power to standards that they and their team have agreed upon. While you might think this means the leader is relinquishing power and control, I have learned that in fact the leader acquires more power to lead the organization and elicits a genuine and personal commitment from everyone else to live up to those standards.

Figure 7 depicts the typical nature of accountability between leaders in an organization: hierarchical.

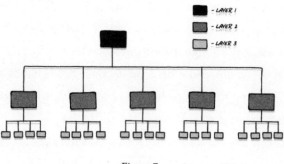

Figure 7

Figure 8 depicts the conceptual shift from accountability through formal hierarchy to a more powerful form of mutual accountability. It's not an accident that figure 8 looks a bit like a snowball.

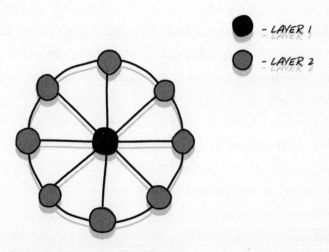

Research and Development by Dr. Peter Fuda, ©2010, All Rights Reserved

Figure 8

The notion of giving up power generally makes leaders uncomfortable, particularly those who rely on their position and title to get things done. But in practice, the chain of command doesn't actually change; subordinates will aspire more willingly to the goals of the leader because they are being led by someone who is holding himself or herself accountable to the same high standards he or she is asking of them.

This can lead to a second concern on the part of the leader: what if my subordinates are perceived as more effective leaders than I am based on the formal ratings in the feedback measure? This was certainly the case for Mike, and is true of many leaders that I have worked with. In reality, absolute ratings are far less important than a leader's commitment to change. What's more, a poor first measure can be a powerful source of leverage for the leader, if used properly. In this respect, a leader can enhance his or her stature with the team or organization simply by demonstrating a high level of commitment and taking actions that demonstrate a clear trajectory toward greater levels of effectiveness.

In Mike's case, at the time of his first feedback session with his executive team, he had three supporters, six quiet detractors, and three vocal detractors within that team. As a result of his display of courage and humility on the day he received his results, he ended the session with six vocal supporters and three who shifted from detractors to a more neutral position. The three who remained detractors following this session increasingly struggled to influence their colleagues. As the Snowball began to roll faster and faster and Mike followed through on his commitment to change, one eventually became a supporter and the other two left the organization.

The key insight for me from this early part of Mike's journey is that his courage and humility became infectious. There was a shift among many members of his team from cynicism to a more empathetic position. Rather than throwing stones at Mike, his team paid more attention to their own weaknesses. And there was an emerging desire to accomplish something important together, as a team.

Motion II—Creating unstoppable momentum

Leadership transformation accelerates as more leaders are swept up by the process. I mentioned earlier that Clynton was the leader who opened my eyes to the power of this phenomenon. In the years since, I have encouraged leaders to embrace the Snowball metaphor systematically and purposefully, and the resulting momentum has often been exponential in scale. Let me tell you a very recent story to illustrate this point further.

Sylvia is the Australian managing director of a leading American fast-moving consumer goods (FMCG) company known around the world for its iconic consumer brands. Her story is instructive for how she mobilized energy and momentum for transformation in her organization.

When I met Sylvia a year into her role, I was struck by her warm, friendly, down-to-earth demeanor. She was not the super-polished kind of leader that I most often meet. This is not to say that she wasn't impressive; quite the opposite: Sylvia was extremely financially literate and acutely aware of the nature of the challenges facing her organization. The company was the clear market leader, but its market share had slowly declined for ten years; a series of aggressive new entrants into the marketplace had begun to leave their mark. On top of this, the company's two largest customers—both supermarket chains—were becoming more and more demanding and putting increasing pressure on costs.

Sylvia was known in her company for being a very passionate and progressive leader; this was a key reason she had been offered the leadership role in the first place. The mandate given to her from headquarters was to halt the market-share decline. This meant leading a turnaround in the company culture, which, to Sylvia's frustration, seemed to be pulling in a different direction.

Despite being a massive global organization, the company retained a very loyal and committed staff. Personnel turnover was very low, and to say that leaders were deeply and emotionally vested in the brands would be an understatement. But this commitment, taken to the extreme, manifested among Sylvia's executive team in two unhelpful ways. The first was in what Sylvia described as a sense of entitlement—leaders felt they needed to be consulted on every decision; unless everyone was consulted, there was little real buy-in, cooperation, or accountability. Second, as a result of this need for consultation, Sylvia's executive team often interfered in operational workflows that their direct reports should have been empowered to manage themselves. This was distracting them from the strategic challenges at hand. Sylvia knew that these tendencies would erode the company's advantage even further if she didn't address them head on.

When Sylvia reached out to me in mid-2011, I was quite perplexed about why she thought she needed my help. She was already a successful change agent, having led a cultural turnaround in her previous role. In fact, I found her to be as literate in the realm of leadership and transformation as any business leader I had worked with. I was even more perplexed when we got her leadership feedback; it revealed that knowing the theory is one thing and putting it into practice on a daily basis under enormous pressure is something altogether different.

Contrary to the very progressive attitudes Sylvia had displayed, her leadership feedback revealed that she was encouraging much of the defensive behavior that she was so frustrated by in her team. Her team reported that she encouraged them to avoid responsibility and depend on her for direction, at the same time as she expected them to stay on top of every detail.

Sylvia was nothing short of dismayed by her feedback: "It was quite devastating," she recalled to me later. "I was meant to be leading and modeling the change. I wanted my team to step up and take more responsibility and be more accountable, and I had been very direct in the feedback I had given to them. And the irony was, I was encouraging them to do the opposite!"

Sylvia wanted the Snowball of change to start rolling as

quickly as possible, and she knew that she had to be the one to set it in motion. She sure didn't like her feedback, but from the word *go*, she took ownership of it. You could say she hurled herself down the mountain. In the debrief session with her team, Sylvia didn't need to be asked to be the first to share — she immediately held her profile up for all to see. She didn't try to rationalize the data or hide her disappointment. But what was most apparent for all to see was her hunger to make a change. With Sylvia demonstrating such openness and vulnerability, her team members were left with no option but to do the same — they all shared their feedback, too. This was the Snowball metaphor in action, right in front of our eyes. But what is truly remarkable is what happened next. Sylvia was about to take her role of modeling change to a whole new level.

Sylvia wanted to better understand her feedback — to move beyond the statistical ratings and get a grasp on what was really going on. She asked me and my colleague Martin to conduct in-depth interviews with her boss, her global peers, and a sample of her direct reports. Given that Sylvia had demonstrated such openness and willingness to learn, the feedback came in thick and fast. One particularly striking piece of feedback came from Sylvia's manager, who indicated that Sylvia was too consumed with what was going on around and below her, and consequently not managing to the needs of the global organization. This was significant because it wasn't too dissimilar from the feedback she had given her own team.

When Sylvia brought her team together and shared her feedback from the interviews, the Snowball picked up speed. She was demonstrating the level of commitment and intensity that she wanted from others, and the team was visibly moved by her resolve. By opening up to her team about the nature of her challenges, Sylvia gained empathy and support from them. They realized that they needed to take their share of responsibility for the company's performance.

To address the two issues of over-consultation and getting too operationally involved, we worked with Sylvia's executive team on a number of important measures. Together, we reviewed their scorecard, which detailed all of the important outcomes they were striving for, in order to clarify who should own what. We identified areas of operational responsibility that could be delegated to the executive team's direct reports. And everybody committed to shared standards of behavior, such as "work together" and "do as you say," which were measured and discussed at every executive-team meeting.

The nature of these commitments had real implications for the next layer of managers in the organization: if the executive team were to get out of operational matters, their direct reports clearly needed to be engaged in the journey as well. In order to achieve this, Sylvia and her team developed a compelling story that drew on people's pride and affiliation with the organization but also defined the changes that everyone needed to make if the organization was to have a vibrant future. The plan was for each member of Sylvia's team to engage their respective teams in this story through face-to-face forums.

At this point, there was some drag on the Snowball. Sylvia was pushing ahead with real passion and energy, but her team did not match her intensity and, pretty soon, they found themselves deferring the storytelling responsibility to her. In a very cathartic conversation, the team realized that their ownership of the transformation journey was being put to the test—and they were failing. It was not Sylvia's role to drive the change; it was everybody's role. The energy this revelation unleashed was enormous. And it created an incredible amount of momentum for the Snowball.

Each of Sylvia's team members ended up not only hosting their own forums and telling the story with passion and conviction, they were also open about their own personal leadership challenges. This helped create a groundswell of commitment among the next layer of managers, who were hungry to engage in the leadership agenda. They were already experiencing less interference and more autonomy, but found the honesty and vulnerability their leaders had demonstrated particularly compelling. In effect, the Snowball of change was now made up of three layers, as represented in figure 9.

The lines of accountability between layers were mutual and worked in multiple directions. The middle layer of the Snowball—the executive team—was accountable not only to Sylvia, but also to one another. What's more, they were now embedded between Sylvia and their highly committed direct reports. This led to a profound shift in the culture of the organization from passivity and reactivity to increased personal initiative and ac-

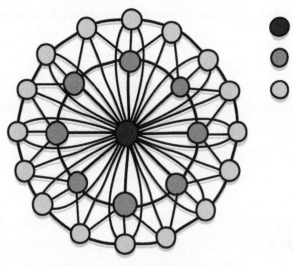

- *LAYER 1*
- *LAYER 2*
- *LAYER 3*

Research and Development by Dr. Peter Fuda. ©2010. All Rights Reserved

Figure 9

countability. One of the best ways to get an indication of an organization's culture is to listen to the conversations taking place in the corridors. More and more often, when my colleague Martin and I roamed the corridor outside Sylvia's office, we heard things along the lines of "We're in charge. We're not going to be the victim. This is our journey."

Eliminating friction and drag

Sylvia's story is a great example of what becomes possible when everyone commits to a shared ambition and an agreed-upon set of leadership standards. But how do you deal with leaders who refuse to embrace those standards and consequently create friction as the Snowball gathers momentum? In my experience, this is a very common (and difficult) challenge for leaders to confront—but also one that can unleash significant force when met in the right way. Paul's experience is a good case in point.

I met Paul, the brand-new managing director of a Dutch IT subsidiary, at his company's annual sales conference. He made a huge impression on me; I had never met a six-foot-eight Elvis impersonator before. Paul had been talked into dressing like Elvis at the conference by a very persuasive colleague who felt that the organization needed some comic relief from its performance woes. Paul was the third managing director in twelve months, and I remember thinking at the time that here was an interesting paradox: the new managing director, with his company in a dire financial situation, dressing in tight, white Lycra in an attempt to connect with his people.

Over the three years we worked together, I came to know Paul as someone with a tough exterior but a very warm and caring center. So it was a real challenge when, a year into his role, Paul was forced to confront the unhelpful behavior of James, one of his key executives.

Paul had realized that a fundamental problem in his organization was poor leadership standards, which translated into a lack of commitment and accountability further down the organization. To address this problem, we worked with Paul and his leadership team to formulate a set of standards to which they would all hold themselves accountable. These standards included "we trust each other," "we deliver," and "we are supportive." In Paul's words, "It would no longer be good enough to get your targets. You now needed to hit your targets and live the agreed standards if you wanted to be considered a success."

Soon after the standards were finalized, it became very clear that Paul's head of service delivery—James—was saying one thing and doing another. In leadership team meetings he talked about the need to increase trust in the organization, and for him and the other executives to be more supportive of their staff. In practice, James often undermined his colleagues behind their backs, and Paul received several complaints from James's staff about his bullying behavior. Hardly the actions of someone committed to trust and support. At best, James was paying lip service to the standards. At worst, he was actively undermining Paul's transformation effort locally and with the parent company. Paul responded initially by getting James a personal coach for regular, intensive sessions, but months went by and nothing changed.

Paul knew that he needed to remove James from the organization, but he hesitated, for several reasons. First, James possessed enormous knowledge about the business and was deeply involved in some key accounts. He also had a strong global network of support in the parent company and was highly regarded for his technical expertise. Finally, there was a strong emotional component to Paul's hesitation: by this stage in his journey, he was an ardent believer in everyone's capacity for change, and he desperately hoped that James could get on board with the transformation agenda. Eventually, though, he ran out of hope and patience: "After all other avenues had been exhausted, I decided to let James go," he later told me. "It was a tough decision but it was necessary for us to move forward. I was surprised by the sense of relief in the organization once the decision had been made. It seemed to unleash a real momentum in key parts of the business."

At some point, almost every leader I have worked with has had to make difficult personnel decisions like this one; and the course of action is particularly challenging when the person creating the friction has a big impact on the organization's financial performance. In nearly all cases, however, the leaders were surprised by the sense of relief and momentum once they had done what they had known needed doing. In fact, I have come to understand that there are few actions more powerful for building momentum for a transformation effort than removing a senior leader who is getting results but causing drag on the Snowball by not living the agreed standards of behavior. Removing this drag or friction is very powerful not just for the organization, but also for the leader who has to make the tough decision. Such an action will be perceived as highly courageous by others, which accelerates the leader's own transformation as well.

The Snowball metaphor teaches us that a leader's personal journey of transformation is contingent upon his or her humility and transparency; effectively, this means there must be a willingness to hold agreed leadership standards above formal authority and hierarchy.

The Snowball is also contingent upon achieving a critical mass of leaders who are mutually accountable to one another and, if necessary, replacing those who are not committed. Finally, the Snowball metaphor compels us to embed shared leadership standards in the organization's systems and structures, such as meetings and performance evaluations. It's at this point that transformation really starts happening — the Snowball becomes almost impossible to stop.

Now what?

If you're action oriented or itching to unleash your Snowball, then I suggest you go to www.peterfuda.com and interact with the Snowball audiovisual tools and exercises before coming back to read the next chapter. If you would prefer to keep reading, or you're not ready for any deep reflection yet, then here are a couple of simple next steps:

- Consider how transparent you are willing to be regarding your challenges and goals.
- Think about how you could get some honest and reliable feedback from those you work with.
- Identify sources of drag or friction in your Snowball and make plans to address them.

3

Master Chef

The Master Chef metaphor is about artfully applying leadership "science"—frameworks, tools, and strategies for change—to help make transformation happen. Over time, leaders can and should advance from amateur cook to master chef, using their skills with increasing creativity and flair and thus maximizing their impact.

THE METAPHOR OF MASTER CHEF may be new to the realm of leadership literature, but it seems particularly apt given the resurgence of interest in cooking in popular culture. Cooking has been elevated to a social phenomenon and a marker of cultural sophistication. Prominent chefs like Jamie Oliver, Wolfgang Puck, Nigella Lawson, and Anthony Bourdain have achieved global celebrity status through their TV shows, restaurants, books, and product endorsements. They exemplify how cooking has become something of a theatrical art form across both old and new media. These chefs work in the culinary arts and draw upon the science of food to artfully create a gastronomic experience that is pleasing to both the palate and the eye.

If we translate this into the context of leadership, it provides extremely valuable insights into transformation. At the most basic level, the Master Chef metaphor helps us understand how a leader can make the transition from being the equivalent of an amateur cook to that of a culinary artist. Leaders must move beyond leadership "science" to a more artful application of change frameworks, tools, and strategies to bring about transformation.

Let's return to Paul, the six-foot-eight managing director (and accomplished Elvis impersonator) of the Dutch IT subsidiary whom we met in the Snowball chapter. Paul cut an imposing figure, and in the early days of his leadership role, he adopted a very dictatorial style of management, almost literally using his size to get things done. It was evident that he felt somewhat inadequate for the role, largely because he had occupied less-scrutinized finance-related positions for the duration of his career and had not received any formal leadership education. What he knew about leadership and carried with him into his new role came largely from his private life: his upbringing, a boarding-school education, and the various sports teams he had been a part of.

Paul was very committed to the leadership transformation agenda we had set for him, and he demanded the same commitment from his team members. In fact, he saw the agenda as a bit of a lifeline; he felt that the transformation process as outlined by me and my colleague Leanne could provide him with the leadership theory and frameworks he sorely needed to do the job well.

Because he had no other reference points, he embraced our change frameworks with a level of discipline and intensity that I had never seen before. This approach included introducing a systematic mix of individual, team, and organizational activities; studying practical strategies to positively change his impact on his colleagues; and making disciplined use of the Leadership/Impact tool.

Being a numbers man, Paul really liked what he perceived to be a very logical, rational, and reliable tool because it made the somewhat foreign concept of leadership seem more scientific; it appealed to his rational nature. He didn't necessarily like the feedback he received — all of which confirmed his overbearing approach — but he accepted it as a snapshot of the reality that others were experiencing. Over time, Paul was able to see how his actions, well-intentioned as they were, were undermining his goal of becoming a highly effective leader.

"The data gave me no place to hide, and my team didn't either," Paul later told me. "They made me aware that I was trying to do it all myself. It was all about 'do it my way' and 'do it today or get out of the organization.' Once I could see it from their point of view, I was in. And if I believe in something, I give it a hundred and fifty percent. It's just my nature."

I found Paul's combination of extreme commitment to a change agenda and a lack of formal leadership education to be a real blessing in the early stages of his journey. Whenever we met for a coaching conversation, he would take copious, detailed notes. He would conclude our meetings by walking to his assistant's desk and asking her to integrate all of his next actions and new commitments into his calendar and task list right there and then in front of me. His uncomplicated and methodical execution gave him great traction very quickly, and gave me the confidence that he would be able to make the changes he had committed to.

So in many ways Paul was a star pupil. The only problem was that his very literal adoption of the leadership science we were providing him with was not necessarily having the kind of impact he desired; the way he went about executing the strategies he wanted to implement often felt stilted. For example, in speaking with staff and customers, Paul could come across as too scripted. When he had to speak off the cuff, he would become very uncomfortable. In fact, whenever things didn't go according to plan, he was lost. This was never more obvious than during his first budget presentation to his global CEO, Karl, at a meeting in Singapore. Karl asked a very specific question about one number, on one line, in one of the many spreadsheets that Paul and his team had prepared. Essentially, the question was designed to try and trip Paul up, and it succeeded. It was at a level of detail that Paul hadn't prepared for and his vague answer didn't satisfy Karl.

"This isn't acceptable," Karl said. "You obviously don't understand your business." Then he walked out of the meeting, embarrassing Paul in front of his international peers. It was a seminal moment in Paul's journey. He felt bullied and humiliated, and all over a fairly minor point that ignored the huge amount of work Paul and his colleagues had done in preparation for the meeting. He got to experience power and control firsthand, and he didn't like it — not one bit.

It was only when he began to link the leadership strategies he was learning to his deeply held values that Paul started to lead more naturally. Paul identified these values as honesty, integrity, and teamwork. He needed to take the science and make it more real and personal in order to fully integrate his insights into his daily interactions. One strategy that resonated with Paul's value of integrity was the idea of *showing* what he wanted from others, as opposed to *telling* them. Despite his size, Paul decided he would only fly economy class, on budget airlines, in order to save his company money. Following Paul's example, nobody at the company asked to fly first-class anymore.

Paul's relationship with his global CEO came full circle a couple of years after that first fateful budget presentation, following a dramatic turnaround in Paul's business. At the company's annual global leadership summit, Karl approached Paul and asked him to share his story of business transformation with the entire forum, a scenario that would have terrified Paul only months earlier, given the high-profile audience and the lack of time to plan his presentation. But he managed to speak off the cuff and from the heart. Despite the significant financial turnaround Paul had achieved, he focused on the transformation he had experienced on a personal level. He talked about how he had shifted from "dictator to disciplined disciple to a more natural leader." He talked about how each member of his executive team had contributed to the turnaround of the business. He went on to link the turnaround in leadership to the success the company had subsequently enjoyed. He told his audience how they had won the prestigious Cisco Technology Excellence Partner of the Year Award. He outlined the lengthy list of new business deals they had won, and only then did he speak about the tremendous turnaround in the financial results. Finally, he thanked Karl for walking out of the presentation in Singapore two years earlier, referring to it as a turning point—which, amusingly enough, Karl mistook for a genuine compliment. When he was done, the global leadership group gave Paul a standing ovation.

Whenever I ask leaders who have shown dramatic improvement in their effectiveness how they did it, I'm usually surprised by their answers. They will almost unanimously point to the frameworks, tools, and strategies we encouraged them to employ. Which is great, of course, but the reason I'm surprised is that there are many frameworks available for those seeking to make changes. The tools and strategies are everywhere, but case studies of transformation are relatively rare. In exploring this seeming paradox, what has emerged for me is a far more nuanced and subtle appreciation of how it is the artful application of frameworks, tools, and strategies that helps leaders transform their leadership and their organizations. It is the Master Chef metaphor that describes this process.

On the following pages, I will break down the Master Chef metaphor into its three constituent parts.

The recipe: Frameworks

To help leaders get a handle on the ever-changing nature of today's business environment, there are hundreds, maybe even thousands of recipes for change available in books, at seminars, online, and elsewhere. Many of these use similar ingredients, such as setting a goal and then laying out a rational, step-by-step program for achieving it. But for me, the methods are far less interesting than the dynamic interaction between instructions on the one hand, and the person using them on the other.

As we saw in Paul's story, the same way that an amateur cook takes comfort from a step-by-step recipe, a business leader—especially one who feels relatively unsophisticated—can take comfort from a carefully crafted framework. By framework, I mean a map of the key activities, time frames, milestones, and commitments on the road to change. The tangible, concrete nature of a framework can be a welcome reference point for leaders as they navigate the somewhat abstract concept of leadership transformation. This was very apparent to me in the story of Dennis, the former actuary and highly intellectual insurance company CEO introduced in the Fire chapter. While Dennis was clearly very committed to his leadership journey, he wasn't particularly comfortable in his role. In fact, at the outset of his journey Dennis was quite daunted by his leadership feedback, which revealed a big gap between his noble vision and how people were actually experiencing him. In his mind, he was entering a new and unknown world, one he did not yet understand and that was a far cry from the concrete actuarial world he was used to.

What enabled Dennis to reach a reasonable degree of comfort was the change framework we provided. When he could see his journey laid out for him in a twelve-month chart across one page, he realized that he didn't have to change overnight. He was at step one, right where he needed to be, and he could see a logical and rational set of steps that would help him make the desired changes over time.

Looking at it this way, Dennis realized he was already on a positive trajectory, and that his initial, fairly negative 360-degree feedback results merely marked a departure point. In the early days, Dennis and I spoke regularly about the importance of trajectory over absolute outcome. He had come from a world where the absolute result was what mattered, so this was an important and empowering distinction for him. The framework provided Dennis with the structure he needed to organize his thinking about how far he had gotten and where he wanted to go next. And since he thrived on intellectual stimulation, his leadership transformation became another interesting challenge to master.

Dennis's initial discomfort is far from unique, and it taught me how much comfort leaders get from a good recipe, especially in times of rapid change. But here's the irony: while most leaders will happily rely on the apparent stability of a clearly defined framework, it is the more fluid and artistic application of that framework to a changing world that really helps accelerate transformation. Just as a chef is constantly altering a recipe depending on the ingredients available, it is important to regularly change the timing, content, or sequence of activities in response to, and in order to capitalize on, the changing nature of a leader's environment.

To illustrate this point, I will turn to Jim, a leader who had been employing different change frameworks for many years before we started working together. Jim was a highly revered director general in the state government of Queensland, Australia. While not a particularly tall man, Jim had enormous presence. What struck me most about Jim at our first meeting was his burgundy bow tie. While most of us struggle to make a bow tie work at a black-tie event, Jim pulled it off in the middle of a working day with ease; it gave him an air of eccentric sophistication.

Jim had a great reputation as a successful change agent within big bureaucracies, having already transformed huge organizations in the Department of Main Roads and the Department of Education. As a lifelong learner and a committed student of management practice, Jim had been experimenting with leadership frameworks, tools, and strategies for more than two decades. But the rubber really hit the road for Jim in his role as director general, where he was tasked with transforming the Department of Primary Industries from an insulated, research-focused organization into an economic powerhouse — a department that would not only do good science, but commercialize that science in a way that benefited the state. It was a challenge that I was excited to partner with Jim on.

About two years into our work together, Jim faced the two toughest challenges of his whole career in quick succession: devastating Cyclone Larry, which caused more than a billion dollars' worth of damage in Northern Australia, and, soon afterward, a deadly outbreak of equine influenza that paralyzed the horse-racing industry across Australia's eastern seaboard, affecting an industry that engages some two hundred fifty thousand Australian workers and has a direct economic benefit of more than seven billion dollars to the national economy.

Given these dramatic changes to Jim's context, with eighteen-hour days now par for the course, it made no sense to work methodically through our previously planned twelve-month framework of leadership activities. Instead, Jim focused on what effective leadership would look like in the midst of these crises and adapted the framework accordingly. Had we stuck to the preplanned framework, the leadership activities would have been theoretical training exercises at best, useless distractions at worst. This experience only confirmed my belief that there is no one best framework for change, and no perfect way to adapt that framework; it must always be understood and approached in its context.

In Jim's case, we shifted from the twelve-month plan to a rolling three-month plan for greater flexibility, held more individual and small-group interactions with key stakeholders instead of the more formal executive-team sessions we had been running, and introduced a monthly town hall meeting with his top leaders to share insights and correct course in real time. The impact on Jim's key stakeholders was powerful: key government ministers supported Jim's efforts, other departments worked closely with his for the first time, and the staff throughout his organization went above and beyond the call of duty to neutralize these crises.

The Queensland government was widely praised for its handling of Cyclone Larry, and contrary to all predictions, Jim's department was able to eliminate equine influenza in Queensland in a little over a year, heading off a national epidemic. In fact, the government's annual report for Jim's department stated that "the success of this response is unprecedented on a world scale, with most observers being skeptical that Australia would ever achieve freedom from equine influenza."

A short time later, as Jim successfully transitioned from career public servant to private-sector CEO at the ripe old age of fifty-five, he was honored with an Order of Australia for his services to government. One could argue that it's only logical that in times of unforeseen crises, previously conceived frameworks need to be adjusted. But one only has to look at the poor response of the U.S. Federal Emergency Management Agency to Hurricane Katrina to realize that this is easier said than done, and that not every leader has the capacity to revise his or her recipe the way Jim did.

The utensils: Tools

Just as chefs can select from many different utensils when creating a dish, business leaders have many tools at their disposal, including ones that profile or measure a range of attributes such as behavior, personality, values, strengths, and thinking styles. While any or all of these tools can be useful in a transformation effort, I have found in my research and practice that it is far more useful to profile a leader's impact than his or her personal attributes. That is, what's most important is how a leader *encourages others to behave.*

The concept of *impact*, as it relates to leadership, was pioneered by Dr. Robert Cooke in the mid-1990s. Unlike behavioral and situational theories of leadership, the idea of impact sits very easily with leaders themselves. In my experience, when leaders get data about the gap between their vision and their impact, they are typically able to create a mental story that allows them to move forward pretty quickly. The gist of what I hear very often is "The data isn't saying I'm a bad person, just that I'm affecting people in ways I don't intend." This is less personal, and difficult to argue with. Here's Tim, the young adver-

tising executive we first met in the Fire chapter: "The data I received was undeniable because it's measuring my impact—it's
saying, 'You may have this wonderful vision, but this is the impact you're having on others.' That's not up for debate; that's
how somebody's experiencing you. It's like Kryptonite to the
ego—it's undeniable."

In the context of impact, a leader's focus can shift quickly
from abstract judgments about "good" or "bad" leadership to
evaluating leadership, in very concrete ways, as being aligned
or misaligned with their vision. For example, you want your
team to work well together, but you constantly compare them to
one another. You desire collaboration, but what you unwittingly
encourage is competition. And unlike approaches that center
on personality, preferences, or values, emotionally charged responses to feedback on impact tend to be less frequent and less
intense.

For a tool to be truly useful in the context of transformation,
of course it needs to be statistically valid and reliable, but also
accessible; it must possess the substance required for credibility
as well as the simplicity required for action. Additionally, a tool
needs to establish a baseline measurement that allows leaders
to see how they are being experienced by their most important
stakeholders—one that allows for an "apples and apples" com-
parison at a point in the future. And that baseline needs to be
set against the leaders' own vision for their leadership.

I also look for tools that can help leaders and their teams establish a shared language for their experience. This shared lan-

guage helps to make the somewhat intangible notion of leadership transformation accessible in their daily interactions. Here, again, is Tim: "A lot of the real richness came in the conversations after we got our leadership data when my team and I started to get a common language; it just gave us a way to talk about it. And even to this day—more than four years after I've been introduced to the tool—me and those around me I've been working with, we still use that language on a day-to-day basis."

Tim's comment hints at the potential of tools to be used in more creative and artistic ways: they might not be—don't even have to be—creative in and of themselves, as long as they enable a shared language from which rich conversations and insights can evolve.

Often tools measure how a leader thinks she is doing at any given moment—this can be valuable in that it can increase self-awareness, but in my experience it can be inadequate for a transformation effort. For example, if a leader knows she is aggressive, and receives data that confirms this, then her key takeaway may be "I'm very self-aware," when really it should be "I'm being too aggressive." Alternatively, if she receives feedback that is worse than her self-perception, her subsequent energy may be spent defending her self-image. Either way, the imperative to change can be sidelined.

If you've read "Read This First" at the start of this book, you will know that the tool I used to baseline the impact of all of the leaders I'm discussing is a 360-degree measurement instrument researched and developed by Human Synergistics International called Leadership/Impact, which you can learn more about in the appendix at the end of this book. Clearly, I am a fan of this tool in the context of leadership transformation and believe it increases the feasibility of success. But to reiterate, a great tool is no guarantee of transformation. To return to the Master Chef metaphor, an amateur chef cannot achieve the same precision with a utensil as someone who has honed his or her technique. Take experienced sushi chefs, who over many years have developed an artful application of their sushi knives. An amateur chef using exactly the same knives is unlikely to replicate their results. They are also unlikely to have a full appreciation of how dangerous these tools can be when used with poor technique!

Let me return to Jim's story to amplify this point, winding back the clock some ten years to a time before he became the Zen-like individual who led his organization through two massive crises. The first time Jim received a piece of leadership feedback as a senior manager was in the early 1990s. It would be an understatement to say that he had a rather emotional reaction: "When the results came in I was shocked. I wanted to kill the bastards that had actually filled in the questionnaire — I wanted to know who they were!"

I was not working with Jim at this time, so it wasn't my life that was in danger. I later learned, however, that Jim's reaction had come in response to a process that lacked context and purpose. Jim thought he was an effective leader. When he received the results of his colleagues' assessment of his leadership, they provided a very different picture of Jim as an extremely aggressive individual. He wasn't given any support or means to create an empowering story around this challenging data, so he internalized it as a personal attack on who he was as a person. He then went on to dismiss the tool as one of those "new-age, fancy tools designed to undermine good managers." Furthermore, he questioned the credibility and integrity of the consultant facilitating the process. Jim's experience reinforced for me how important it is that any tool, no matter how well designed, must be artfully applied in order to be effective.

One leader I had the privilege of working with, and who leveraged the ideas in the Master Chef metaphor in her transformation, was Vicki. I got to know her after she had been appointed the new head of an $8 billion superannuation and investments business in a publicly listed insurance company. As a young, pregnant female executive in an industry traditionally dominated by middle-aged men, Vicki certainly broke the mold. This was probably not a bad thing given the state of the business, which was under enormous pressure to maintain historical profit margins in the face of increasingly aggressive competitors. Internally, the business had developed a reputation as being an island within the organization—detached, disintegrated—and, worse still, as being competitive with the company's other business units.

By the time Vicki returned from maternity leave, both of these problems had worsened and very quickly threatened to consume her, creating stress and tension in her personal and professional life. In our work with Vicki, tools became very significant for her, and she applied them artfully to her challenges. Her leadership feedback showed that while Vicki had a constructive impact overall, her impact on her peers — the heads of the other business units — was poor. This was a wake-up call for Vicki because she knew she could not be successful on her own; she needed the support of her colleagues. Vicki met this challenge by using her feedback to address not just her impact on her peers, but as a way to open a dialogue with them about how to better reintegrate her business into the company as a whole.

Vicki was inspired to apply the findings from the feedback process to the very fabric of her personal and professional life, and underwent a deep exploration of her most important roles and priorities. Personally, her priorities were her young family and increasing her energy. Professionally, her main priority was to calm the frenzy that had engulfed the business in her absence.

In their foundational work, *The Leadership Challenge: How to Make Extraordinary Things Happen in Organizations*, renowned leadership scholars James Kouzes and Barry Posner speak about the important signals leaders send with how they spend their time: "How you spend your time is the single clearest indicator of what's important to you . . . Visibly spending time on what's important shows you're putting your money where your mouth is. Whatever your values are, they have to show up in your calendar and on meeting agendas for people to believe that those values are significant."

Vicki enlisted her executive assistant to translate her priorities into her calendar. Meetings and tasks were accepted or rejected accordingly, and regular tracking—in the form of simple statistics—allowed Vicki to recognize where her efforts were aligned with her priorities and address where they weren't. She used these statistics to engage her team, both practically and symbolically, in what was important to her. She could show them, for example, that her goal to spend more time focused on the customer was being hampered by internal bureaucracy and countless meetings. In this sense, I consider Vicki to have used the tools at her disposal both scientifically and artfully; that is, despite her systematic and disciplined approach, Vicki did not simply use them to engage in the process we were running in her organization, but as a catalyst to transform her organization and her life. She used the tools to increase the balance in her life, the quality of her relationships, and her overall sense of happiness and satisfaction.

In Vicki's words: "Being a master chef requires you to perfect and continuously refine your own techniques so you can demonstrate them to others—not through telling, but through your own personal actions and role-modeling. And like all chefs, this is harder to do under stress and pressure, but that's when it's most important to employ these techniques. You need to achieve mastery so it becomes intuitive to do in tough circumstances."

Things shifted for Vicki in the following months. She reduced her stress levels and became more focused on the things that mattered at work. Both of these shifts allowed her to spend more time with her young family, and be fully present when she was with them. The frenzy that she had found when she returned from maternity leave gave way to a much simpler and more focused agenda for her team. Over time, Vicki's drive to simplify her organization yielded significant results; she was able to cut cost inefficiencies by 20 percent and maintain historical profit margins at a time when the industry as a whole was becoming less profitable. In fact, she was so successful with her simplification agenda that her boss asked her to take what she had learned and apply it across the whole company in a role of increased scope and influence.

The cooking methods: Strategies

While a framework provides leaders with a plan and creates a sense of comfort, and tools supply data and a language for change, leaders still need to implement actions in order to transform their effectiveness. This is where strategies come in; within the Master Chef metaphor, they are the equivalent of cooking methods such as steaming or frying.

There are many strategies in the literature that leaders can use to increase their effectiveness. In fact, the Leadership/Impact tool presents ten very well-researched strategies. My goal here is not to provide a detailed rundown, classification, or examination of leadership strategies in general. Rather, I want to highlight the strategies that the leaders in this book used to become more effective. At the highest level, the biggest shift made by every leader in this book was the surrender of absolute control in favor of a more empowering and collaborative approach to leadership.

In my research and practice, I have found that the seemingly simple notion of giving up control is actually a considerable challenge for most leaders. I believe the reason for this is a false assumption: that the opposite of control is chaos — something most leaders wish to avoid at all costs. But the opposite of total control isn't chaos at all; it is simply creating a context where autonomy and accountability are in balance.

Too much autonomy without sufficient accountability can result in chaos, to be sure. But too much accountability without sufficient autonomy creates resentment and a sense of helplessness because subordinates can be held responsible for outputs when in reality they don't own the inputs.

I learned the lesson of autonomy and accountability very early in my life — in fact, it's my earliest childhood memory. As a seven-year-old, I tried to use the excuse of a mild cold one winter morning to skip a day of school. "Don't go to school for me," my mother told me. "It's not my education. You need to make your own choices in life." Her strategy was clever, and very effective: I got out of bed, went to school, and have had a strong sense of personal accountability for my decisions ever since. I'm sure it's one reason I'm so passionate about this idea today.

The leaders I've worked with have used several strategies to successfully give up control and achieve a healthy balance between autonomy and accountability. Ken, the head of finance and administration for a division of a publicly listed construction company, serves as a good example for some of these strategies in action.

We had begun working with Ken's company just a few months before he transferred from another division within the organization. The business had poor financial performance and a senior team that was in disarray and under pressure from its shareholders. Unlike his predecessor, who had been outspoken and direct, Ken struck me as thoughtful and introverted. He was a smart numbers guy who, by his own admission, "worked inside the finance box and wasn't very strategic." Ken's leadership feedback only served to reinforce my perception; it showed that he was encouraging conventional thinking — driving his team to follow the rules and think inside the box. In subsequent conversations, Ken articulated a desire to break out of this box. It was clear to him, and to his general manager, that he had a critical role to play in the turnaround of the business and that a new approach was needed.

In practice, the first thing Ken did was articulate to his team and colleagues a new purpose for his role. No longer would the primary focus be on control and "rear-view-mirror" financial reporting. He wanted his team to become advisors to the leaders of the company's individual construction projects, to provide them with the insight and information required to better plan and manage their business, anticipate problems, and maximize their performance.

To this end, Ken worked with the project directors to develop a detailed scorecard for each of the projects and for the business as a whole. At every leadership meeting, he shared the latest results and pointed out emerging trends. He became very skilled at asking open-ended questions of his audience so that they were encouraged to explore the data. This resulted in his colleagues looking for opportunities and potential problems — and ultimately taking ownership of them.

And Ken didn't stop with the company's senior leaders: he accompanied his GM on all of his town hall meetings with staff and shared the same data with them. The goal was to encourage ownership of the numbers across the company and to initiate a change in its culture toward greater openness and transparency. Ken's strategy worked — his presentations became a source of real anticipation and conversation among all levels of staff.

In spite of his natural introversion, Ken invested heavily in building relationships with his senior colleagues in an effort to address the mistrust that had built up over the years between his division and the project teams. This investment resulted in Ken and his team becoming critical and valued members of the project teams. Where once their role had been to grill project teams on the granular details of their financial results and conduct postmortems on projects gone wrong, now the finance team was at the table from the very beginning and could use its skills and insights to set projects up for success.

As Ken's stature increased, he began to transcend the role he had originally been appointed to. He became the key advisor to his GM, and was asked to oversee all the company's strategic business initiatives. At a recent leadership meeting, he was overwhelmingly recognized by his peers as the leader who had made the biggest contribution to strategic conversations within the business.

Ken helped his business to increase its volume of client work by 173 percent and revenue by 113 percent. Staff turnover dropped to half the industry average, and the company became a leader in safety.

Let's take a more detailed look at some of the strategies I have found to be fundamental to a leader's ability to move away from control and toward a more empowering approach to leadership. The five strategies that I outline below are based, in part, on my observation of how the leaders in this book applied the Leadership/Impact strategies that I mentioned earlier. To reinforce the idea of "frying less and steaming more," I present these strategies as "from–to."

Strategy one: from content to context. Leaders shift their focus from the day-to-day operational and technical detail of their world to creating a context for the success of others. This means defining or redefining the purpose of their leadership, their team, and their organization, articulating what success looks like, setting boundaries, and determining the standards that will guide their behavior as they pursue their purpose and goals. In Ken's case, this involved redefining his company's finance function from auditing to providing services and expertise.

Strategy two: from talking to walking. Leaders shift from telling others what is required to showing them. As Kouzes and Posner write in *The Leadership Challenge*, "Sometimes the greatest distance we have to travel is the distance from our mouths to our feet." This is certainly true in my experience. One of the challenges in synchronizing our words and our actions is what social psychologists call "illusory superiority," a cognitive bias that causes us to overestimate our positive abilities and underestimate our negative ones. This may be why 93 percent of us believe we are above-average drivers! In practical terms, the leaders in this book sent a clear message to their organizations that they were practicing what they were preaching. Ken didn't just talk about transparency, he showed everyone the numbers.

Strategy three: from competing to collaborating. This shift involves moving from isolation, politics, and interpersonal conflict toward genuine relationships built on trust and a desire for mutual success. The best way I know to build trust is to extend more trust than is warranted, and each of the leaders in this book did just that. Ken got out of his office and visited with the project leaders. He listened to their concerns, responded to their needs, and set goals that bound his team's success to theirs.

Strategy four: from guru to guide. Here, leaders shift from providing answers to coaching others to find answers for themselves. A simple formula we use with leaders, adapted from American psychologist Norman R. F. Maier, is ED = Q x O: an Effective Decision is the product of the Quality of that decision and its Ownership by others. In discussions with his team members, rather than provide all of the answers as he saw them, Ken used open-ended questions as well as moments of silence to coax his colleagues out of their previously passive or aggressive positions into ones where they felt like they owned the outcome.

Strategy five: from critic to cheerleader. This final strategy involves moving from a focus on what is going wrong to what is going right. Of course, shining a light on issues and problems is an important part of transformation, but it must not become a leader's default setting. An important mantra in my life, given to me by an early mentor and which I have shared with almost every leader I have ever met, is "Don't let perfect get in the way of better." This is critical when you are trying to build momentum for change. In his famous scorecard updates, Ken did present the brutal facts, but he spent more time highlighting the positive trend lines and drawing attention to the efforts of the people in the room who were causing the numbers to shift in the right direction.

Just as a chef cooks with more flair, creativity, and spontaneity as his technique becomes second nature, leaders can become less rigid and more intuitive over time. To quote the legendary French chef Marcel Boulestin, "Cookery is not chemistry. It is an art. It requires instinct and taste rather than exact measurements."

As I mentioned early on in this chapter, an abundance of frameworks, tools, and strategies are readily available for those seeking to bring about change; yet stories of successful transformation are relatively rare. In the highly volatile environments of the leaders that I have worked with, I have found no precise formula, and no sequence of predictable steps, that will guarantee success. This is not to downplay the leadership science. There are certain techniques that must be mastered before a cook can begin to unleash his or her creativity and intuition, and following recipes meticulously can be a good starting point. But in order to effect leadership transformation, it is essential to move beyond the science to a more artful application of the frameworks, tools, and strategies to respond to the unique, ever-changing context of a leader's journey.

Now what?

If you're action oriented or ready to get cooking, then I suggest you go to www.peterfuda.com and interact with the Master Chef audiovisual tools and exercises before coming back to read the next chapter. If you would prefer to keep reading, or you're not ready for any deep reflection yet, then here are a couple of simple next steps:

- Think about whether you could use frameworks and tools more artfully.
- Consider which of the five leadership strategies you are strong in, and which ones need more of your focus.
- Apply one strategy this week, and reflect on the impact it has on your colleagues.

4

Coach

The Coach metaphor describes how a coaching staff can collectively help leaders achieve their aspirations. It is not about leaders becoming coaches; it's about leaders letting themselves be coached by others — consultants, colleagues, even family members.

ACCORDING TO THE MERRIAM-WEBSTER *Dictionary,* the word "coach" is derived from the Hungarian *kocsi,* a type of large wagon used to transport passengers. The metaphorical extension of the *kocsi,* or "coach" as it was translated into English, is a person who transports people from a state of ignorance to one of knowledge. The use of the word to represent a trainer or teacher surfaced around 1830 at Oxford University to signify a tutor who "carried" a student through an exam.

Today, coaching is used in a wide range of professional disciplines including business, education, and psychology. When you think about coaching in these contexts, the image that probably comes to mind is a one-to-one consultation that takes place behind closed doors, detached from the usual work environment. In contrast, our research led me to explore the use of the word within the context of sport and how that somewhat different use applies to leadership transformation.

Geoff was the CEO of a wealth-management business within a giant corporation. Geoff was also Vicki's boss—Vicki being the young superannuation executive we met in the Master Chef chapter. Geoff rose steadily in the financial services sector before being headhunted for this first CEO role in his mid-forties. He certainly looked and sounded the part; I found him to be a polished and intelligent executive. Unfortunately, his excitement at landing the big job didn't last long. He started in May 2008, just a few short months before the financial crisis nearly wiped out his organization.

I had also worked with Geoff's predecessor, Dennis, whom we first met in the Fire chapter. As a result, Geoff and I met very early in his tenure, while he was reviewing his new business. I liked him from the beginning. Beyond his obvious intelligence, he was also curious and demonstrated real integrity. In my experience, it's typical for a new CEO to criticize their predecessor's work in order to score cheap points with their stakeholders. But Geoff was interested in what he should keep, not just in what he should change now that he was in charge.

The good feeling I had about Geoff seemed to be mutual, so we began meeting over coffee every few weeks. Geoff used our sessions to test and shape his thinking about his business and its people, something he didn't feel he could do with his colleagues at the outset, given that he was a new CEO who hadn't come from within the organization. For my part, I was very keen to help keep the Snowball rolling in Geoff's business. I had invested heavily in Dennis and his team in previous years, and I shared Dennis's desire to leave a legacy of successful performance. So Geoff and I began an informal coaching relationship in which I drew on my knowledge of his business and team to reinforce, push back on, or challenge him about the potential consequences of his ideas and decisions.

Geoff later told me that these early conversations, which happened for several months before we engaged formally in late 2008, were critical in establishing trust for our future relationship. He said that I had behaved with real integrity by "telling him the truth" regardless of how challenging that truth might be for him. Geoff meant by this that I was prepared to risk upsetting or offending him by questioning assumptions or ideas that I felt — from my vantage point — might harm the business or achieve a poor outcome. He came to see my intent as largely free of self-interest.

It was just as well that I had developed this level of trust with Geoff, because the environment after the financial crisis became extremely challenging for him and for his business. He responded to it by becoming very task-focused at the expense of his relationships, trying to do it all himself. Geoff's impact suffered — his team lost confidence and his new boss, Phillip, found Geoff to be lacking in focus and clear direction. All of this tension came to a head when Phillip called Geoff in for a crucial conversation one year after Geoff had taken the reins.

"I don't know if this is going to work between you and me," Phillip announced. By the time Geoff arrived at my office for his next one-on-one, he was in a state of mild panic. In his own words: "I knew my job was on the line and I was catastrophizing the situation. You calmed me down and forced me to look at the world from Phillip's perspective — to look at the facts objectively. I wasn't giving Phillip what he needed as the group CEO. In order to satisfy our investors, he needed to know I was on top of my business, that I had a solid plan. Instead, I was reacting to him and projecting confusion."

It was clear that Geoff needed a way of communicating with Phillip that would project a calm focus on the things that were most important, something to help him navigate his way out of a very complex and high-risk situation. He needed a playbook. So that's what he and I set out to develop.

First, we developed a one-page plan based on the five result areas important to Phillip. It rated each area, gave reasons for each rating, and identified next actions. This on-the-spot analysis helped Geoff get an instant picture of where he was in the game, and showed him how he could play a much better second half.

Every month, Geoff updated the plan and sent it to Phillip in advance of their one-on-one meeting. He would then begin each meeting by highlighting what was going well and subsequently addressing problem areas, detailing all the corrective actions he and his team were taking. He would then very openly ask Phillip whether there was anything else he should or could be doing. This shift allowed Phillip to play a very strong coaching role with Geoff, providing him with insights and suggestions from his own experience. Over time, Phillip moved from being Geoff's provocateur to becoming a real supporter and advocate for him and his business.

Although I was a consultant to Geoff, I operated more like a sports coach — he needed help defining the plays that would let him and his team deal with the complex environment they were operating in. I was able to draw on my experiences in similar situations with other leaders to help Geoff play a strong second half.

In sports, the head coach usually does not work in isolation. There is an entire coaching staff that works closely with the players on different aspects of the game, both offense and defense. The same is true when you apply the Coaching metaphor to business. Concurrently with our one-on-one coaching sessions and his monthly sessions with Phillip, Geoff was also engaged in monthly peer coaching with a couple of his team members.

The members of Geoff's peer coaching group were not, strictly speaking, his peers — they were two of his team members: Vicki, the executive in charge of the superannuation business, and Liz, Geoff's executive officer. Each month, Geoff, Vicki, and Liz would meet not as superior and subordinates, but as equals. They would discuss how they were each progressing toward their leadership goals, and the strategies they were using. Sometimes my colleague Graham facilitated these sessions, and at others the team got together informally and worked alone. They talked about how they had handled various business situations over the previous month, and how they intended to deal with those on the horizon for the next month. Then they shared insights and advice with each other.

In one memorable session in mid-2011, with the tough economic outlook showing no signs of recovery, Geoff shared his intention to simplify the cost structure of the business and reduce the amount of capital on the balance sheet. In order to reap the economic benefit of these actions and satisfy the shareholders, Geoff had to move quickly. Vicki and Liz were concerned that Geoff's urgency could disengage his executive team members, who were critical to implementing the necessary actions. They counseled Geoff that, rather than simply telling everyone what was required and demanding immediate compliance, he should provide the information and insight that would help the team see that their cost structure and capital allocation were too big relative to the size of their business, given the slowing economy. He could then ask the team for their recommendations to address these issues. Geoff embraced Vicki and Liz's advice with great effect; his team took ownership of the two issues and quickly implemented solutions that gave Geoff the fast payoff he needed.

There is something to be said for the value of such on-the-field coaching. These sessions gave Geoff insights that the formal coaching staff — myself and Graham — weren't able to provide. Because of Vicki and Liz's proximity to Geoff and their sheer volume of day-to-day interaction, they were able to give him real-time insights that he could put into practice immediately. They helped Geoff integrate the leadership theory he was learning into his leadership practice. They pointed out both what he was doing well and where his blind spots were. Geoff found these sessions hugely valuable.

The very composition of this peer coaching team — Vicki and Liz being Geoff's direct reports — sent a strong message to the rest of the group that he valued learning over hierarchy.

But the Coaching metaphor can be taken further still; beyond the coaching staff are the fans. For Geoff, his most important fan has always been his wife, Henrietta. To those who know her, Henrietta is a wonderfully authentic and expressive woman. Geoff and Henrietta married in 2007, bringing together a *Brady Bunch* of seven fantastic kids in the process; anyone who comes into their world — as I have on occasion — cannot help but be inspired by their spirit.

In sports, fans cheer their team on and offer encouragement, but they also express their displeasure when players underperform. In Geoff's journey, Henrietta has played this role with passion and enthusiasm. Geoff has told me many times that he would not be where he is today without Henrietta. She has encouraged him to open up to life's experiences and has helped him be "more open, more relaxed, and less formal." She has also pushed him to fulfill his potential and challenged him to pursue his professional ambitions with vigor, all the while ensuring that he remains very connected with what is most important in life: his family and friends.

Henrietta and I have spoken often about Geoff's journey. In fact, all three coaching groups—me, Henrietta, and Vicki, Liz, and Graham—have had very open conversations with each other, encouraged by Geoff. In Geoff's mind, this coherent and supportive approach to his coaching has been "a very important factor in my personal happiness and professional success." Since taking the CEO role, Geoff has transformed his own leadership effectiveness. This is evidenced not just by his 360-degree feedback results, but by the confidence his boss and his team have in him. Under Geoff's leadership, his business emerged from the 2008 financial crisis not just intact, but with record levels of profit, customer satisfaction, and employee engagement.

Professional athletes receive coaching from a variety of sources beyond their head coach. This coaching happens in public as well as private settings. Both of these aspects of coaching apply in a business context and, as I've said before, it's important to understand that the Coach metaphor is not about leaders becoming a coach. It is about how they enable themselves to be coached by others.

In my research and consulting work, I was first encouraged to use the notion of Coach as it applies to sports through a conversation with Paul — the six-foot-eight Elvis impersonator — who has a penchant for comparing leadership and football. When Paul says football, he means rugby, but it could apply just as easily to American football. Given my Italian heritage, when I say it, I mean what Americans call soccer — a truly international sport that is played by men and women at the highest level in every corner of the globe.

Football metaphors are, of course, not new in leadership literature, and are often related to individualistic and competitive behaviors. My interpretation, however, is quite different: for me, football is a team sport. Teams comprised of superstars often lose to cohesive teams of individually inferior players. While a business leader may be seen to be the captain of a team, there is an important distinction to be drawn between the role of captain and coach. While the captain may have been selected for the role because of a certain leadership quality he or she displays, a captain cannot be successful without support from the team.

Paul got me thinking that any successful football team requires a clear distribution of roles both within and around the team, and this distribution of functions seemed similar to those assumed by the groups who can help a business leader transform, as illustrated in Geoff's story: a formal coaching staff, such as consultants or executive coaches; teammates, such as the leader's peer group and direct reports; and fans, such as family members who are vested in the leader's performance.

All of the leaders in this book have used some combination of these three distinct groups. I now want to explore each of them for you, and the roles associated with them, drawing again on both my academic research and my consulting work.

The coaching staff

One of the key elements leaders value about me and my "coaching staff" is that we provide them with solid, tried-and-tested leadership expertise, or what I referred to in Geoff's story as the playbook—a set of strategies a team can follow in order to succeed in a given situation. The assumption is that the suggested strategy has worked before in a similar context. The leaders I've worked with wanted access to a proven set of plays that would help them avoid common mistakes and accelerate their success.

From the research, it became very clear that what these leaders valued even more than the playbook itself was help putting its strategies into action. As the legendary basketball coach and bestselling author John Wooden once said, "A coach is someone who can give correction without creating resentment." Over the years, many leaders have told me that receiving very direct and honest feedback has been a crucial part of their transformation.

Here's the challenge: direct feedback is something that most leaders say they want, but rarely receive. This is because, in practice, truly direct feedback can be pretty scary for a coach to give, and often terrifying for a leader to openly receive. To help you better understand this dynamic, and encourage you to seek this kind of feedback, I'm going to provide a detailed example — one that held a lot at risk for me and for the leader.

Let's return to Tim, the young-gun advertising executive in the early stages of his leadership role whom we met in the Fire chapter. Tim credits some very direct coaching interventions we had as instrumental in shifting his motivation away from the burning platform that had engulfed his life and toward a burning ambition. "The power of those interventions was that you really inserted yourself in my mind quite directly, and it was very interruptive to my bad habits," he later told me. "I honestly believe that if left to my own devices, it would have taken me somewhere between fifteen years and my entire life to make the changes that those interventions created in a couple of profound giant strides."

At the start of our work together, Tim was so committed to making positive changes in his life that he asked me to do whatever it took to hold him accountable to his vision for effective leadership and help him fulfill his purpose to "live a big and authentic life." I cannot overemphasize how big a moment this was in our coaching relationship — this was my chance to establish what "hold me accountable" meant to Tim. I asked him if this meant that he wanted me to give him very direct feedback when I saw him get off course, or whether he would prefer a more warm and cuddly approach. Tim was adamant that I should do the former; "The more direct the better," he said.

I soon had the opportunity to test Tim's resolve. I remember vividly the day Tim came running to see me just before he was due to address his senior staff on the vision and future strategy of the agency. He was stuck on his introduction for the talk and wanted to bounce his thoughts off me. At the time, Tim was about thirty pounds heavier than he is today. He was sweating, his tie was skewed, and he was still huffing and puffing from his run up the stairs as he launched into what felt like an incoherent series of thoughts and ideas.

The high stakes and urgency of the situation encouraged me to be very direct with him. I was worried he was going to project chaos to his team, and I also recognized this as a seminal moment in our coaching relationship. After all, Tim had asked me to be direct when he got off track with his vision, and this was as off-track as I had ever seen anybody. If I failed to deliver what I had promised to him, not only would it represent a missed opportunity on Tim's journey, but it could also seriously undermine his trust in me and in our relationship. All of these factors encouraged me to put my anxiety to one side and tell him what he needed to know.

I reminded Tim of my commitment to him — that I would call him out whenever I saw him off track. Then, calling on all my resolve, I told him that this was one of those moments. I asked him to take a long, hard look at himself. I told him that he did not resemble the kind of leader he aspired to be, and that if I were a member of his team, given the chaos he was projecting, I would be unlikely to follow him around the corner, let alone into the bright future of the company he was trying to sell.

Tim looked shell-shocked. His eyes widened, he sucked in a

long breath, and took a big step back. The few seconds of silence that followed felt like an eternity, and I was genuinely unsure about what might happen next. To my relief, Tim finally breathed out and gave me a half smile. Then he looked down at himself as if to check my assessment of the situation, before thanking me for being honest with him and preventing what was sure to have been a disaster. As he started to fix his appearance, we talked about what he might say in his introduction and how he could deliver it in a compelling way—one that would ease him into the situation and inspire confidence in his staff. In this calmer state, he was able to access his considerable passion and intellect, and then to deliver one of his most inspiring speeches.

Though this kind of coaching may seem overly direct and confrontational, in my experience, it can dramatically accelerate a leader's transformation. It can disrupt unhelpful patterns, save leaders' time and energy by getting straight to the heart of the matter, and represent a powerful learning experience for the journey ahead.

If you ever sign up for this kind of coaching—which I encourage you to do—there are some important conditions to consider in order for it to be well received. As with Tim, permission to provide direct coaching should always be established before it is given; once again, something I encourage you to do with your coaches. Personally speaking, I feel that this principle is so critical that I write it into the contracts I make with my clients.

As a leader, one of the things to look for in a coach is someone with whom you can establish very high levels of trust—a principle that is absolutely fundamental to the type of coaching I am advocating here. Trust is one of those concepts that can mean different things to different people. Some people describe it as a feeling. For example, one thing I have heard from many leaders over the years is "I can't quite put my finger on it, but I just don't trust him." This kind of gut response isn't very helpful for a leader or their coach, though, so based on my experiences, both good and bad, I have developed the following three-part description for trust: perceived credibility, demonstrated reliability, and assumed good intent in the eyes of the audience. I'll now break down these three elements of trust, sharing with you examples from my own experience of trying to build it with clients.

Credibility is like the résumé. The first question we generally think about when we are deciding whether we can trust someone — in a business context, at least — is "Do I believe you can do what you say you can?" For this, we look for evidence of previous results and referrals from people we already trust.

All of the leaders I have worked with found their way to me through one of three primary channels: referrals from another leader who had successfully worked with my company, a speaking engagement where I was positioned as an expert, or through some form of media or high-profile publication such as the *Harvard Business Review*. Then, once they had checked out my credentials, they found more evidence and stories that helped paint a picture of me and my company as competent and credible change agents. By the time I met each leader for the first time, they'd already assumed I knew what I was doing, so we came to the table as equals trying to figure out if we were a good fit for one another.

Next, reliability is like the proof point for our credibility, harder both to earn and to maintain. The question on our mind here is "Do you actually deliver what you say you will?" We look for examples of where a person's promises translate into actions, and where their potential manifests itself into concrete results.

Having established a level of perceived credibility with the leaders you're encountering in this book, I then had to match my delivery to their expectations. My belief is that this developed through many interactions with each leader over several years; a combination of big moments and small ones. In the big moment with Tim above, my direct coaching not only helped put him back on track toward his vision, it also demonstrated that I would deliver on my commitments even in the most difficult and personally risky situations.

Even though credibility and reliability are, to some extent, subjective concepts, I have found ways I could make them more tangible. For example, suggesting a leader review a subordinate's previous performance evaluations to see if they habitually deliver on what they promise. Somewhat more difficult to classify in my trust definition is the notion of assumed good intent, yet I believe this is the most important element underpinning the trust between a coach and a leader. The questions in our mind when we think about good intent are "What is your motivation here? What do you stand to gain? How much of the real you do I see, and how much is a performance?"

Thinking about this concept of assumed good intent, I am reminded of a time some years ago when I was trying to quantify why most of my business partnerships were mutually successful, while a few ended in tears for me or the other party. I developed a simple, four-quadrant grid (figure 10) to help make sense of this question. The horizontal axis indicates "values" in the sense of an alignment of two parties' beliefs and assumptions. The vertical axis indicates "value" in the sense of the likely return on effort or investment for both parties.

What I found was that I had intuitively steered clear of any relationships in Quadrant 2, Strangers, with a low alignment of both values and value. Quadrant 1, Friends, with a high values and low value alignment, either contained leaders I had worked with previously whom I liked to stay in contact with, or leaders I had met and with whom I shared similar values and beliefs, but without our having yet found a way to add commercial value to one another at that particular time.

I found that the few partnerships that ended poorly were in Quadrant 3, Users, with a low values and a high value alignment. These partnerships looked good on the surface because of the apparent rewards for either party, but inevitably became very hard work and highly transactional in nature. Quadrant 4, Partners, was where all my successful partnerships were, and therefore every case of true leadership transformation I have been a part of. To quote a cliché, there was a win-win for both

The Values / Value Alignment Grid©

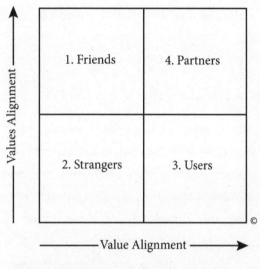

Figure 10

Research and Development by Dr. Peter Fuda. ©2010. All Rights Reserved

the leader and myself. As I reflect now on all of the leaders in this book, each of them was in Quadrant 4, Partners, for the duration of our formal engagements, and Quadrant 1, Friends, when we were not formally engaged.

The reason these leaders trusted my intent is because we were always values-aligned and only ever engaged in commercial activities when there was a real value exchange to be had. For example, Geoff was in the Friends quadrant for many months before we both felt comfortable that there was a viable exchange of value for our organizations that would move us into the Partners quadrant. The need to find a value alignment was always a very transparent and pragmatic conversation with each of the leaders in this book, and I believe it perpetuated the high levels of trust in my intentions that allowed me to give them very direct coaching.

Teammates and the value of on-field coaching

Returning to the arena of sports once more, a team captain's success is generally dependent upon the support of his or her teammates. Realizing this helps extend our understanding of the Coach metaphor from the idea of two people behind closed doors to a dynamic situation involving many people in both planned and spontaneous interactions.

At a practical level, leaders spend far more time with their teams than they do with their external coaches. A leader's team can be a vital source of motivation, feedback, and insights, as it was for Geoff with Vicki and Liz. Interaction with subordinates in this way requires significant trust and respect from each party, and a great deal of humility on the part of the leader.

In Geoff's case, the group coaching relationship was between leader and subordinates, or, to stay within the metaphor, between captain and teammates. In my experience, it can work equally well with teammates at the same level, on one condition: success is dependent on having agreed-on principles among the members for how the peer coaching will work; what we might call contracting principles. I want to illustrate this point with the example of a peer group relationship that developed in an Italian eyewear and eye care multinational. The organization was led by Chris, the company's Asia-Pacific CEO, whom we will reencounter in the Russian Dolls chapter. Chris is not the focal point of this story, but he was truly supportive of the peer coaching process I'm going to describe.

One peer coaching group in Chris's organization included the directors of marketing, product, and operations. This group came together with the explicit aim of exploring the various leadership strategies they were each working on. Though each member was open, constructive, and engaged in the sessions, the group was not getting real traction at first.

Discussing the problem with my colleague Ian — their external coach — it became apparent to the group that they lacked a set of agreed-on principles to make their meetings a success. The first question Ian put to the group was "Have you established clear outcomes for the peer coaching relationship you have entered?" The answer was no; the group had come together with good intentions but only vague ideas about what they each wanted to gain from the process. The second question was "When you present your progress to your colleagues, do you have specific questions that you are looking for them to answer?" Again the answer was no; following each leader's progress report, the group would commence a conversation without any real focus or direction. Sometimes this was useful; at other times it just went around in circles. The third question was "Have you agreed on the behavioral standards that you will all abide by in these sessions?" Yet again, the answer was no.

To address these gaps, the group decided to develop a peer coaching agreement that spoke to their individual and collective expectations. They each identified how they would like to be supported by their peer coaches, and they defined the behaviors that they would abide by in giving and receiving feedback, including principles of honesty, consideration of one another's time, and confidentiality.

As a result the group's sessions became a lot more outcome-focused. On any given topic, members were now very clear about whether they were looking to their colleagues for specific feedback, to hold them accountable for the changes they had committed to, or to just play the role of sounding board for an idea.

For example, one participant said, "When I present my progress report, you will see that I'm still struggling with delegating responsibility to my direct reports. I really need some effective strategies in this area, and would appreciate any thoughts you might have about where I can improve, along with ideas from your own experience."

Over time, this small-group experience became quite cathartic for its members. It functioned like a confessional where they could unburden themselves and get multiple brains working on the leadership issues they found somewhat challenging.

The team became very proficient at giving and receiving helpful feedback. And in being vulnerable and courageous within the group, each member enlisted the others as supportive coaches. The result of these interactions was to uncover blind spots for each other, and to increase the clarity and commitment for each member about what they needed to change.

This is very similar to what coaching experts Marshall Goldsmith, Andrew Thorn, and Marilyn McLeod talk about in their paper, "Peer Coaching Overview." For peer coaching to be impactful, each coach plays three basic roles for the other, expressed as: I'm your thinking partner, I'm here as objective support, and I'm here to help you be accountable.

While peer coaching is clearly very powerful when it emerges informally, there are also ways to encourage such relationships to develop through formally designed interactions and interventions. With every leader in this book, we ran whole-team group coaching sessions at least every quarter. The group coaching forums provided a relatively safe and structured environment for team members to offer coaching to each other based on insights they had accumulated through frequent interaction and close observation. These formal sessions encouraged team members to give feedback informally at other times as well. One particularly memorable example comes from Alan, whom we met in the Fire chapter: "My HR director, Glen, told me that I talked too much and listened too little, that I was always pitching and selling my ideas. I told him to do whatever it takes to stop me doing this. The next day he brought in a roll of gaffer tape and put it on the table in a management meeting. I got the message."

Alan's quote illustrates how feedback offered in a formal group coaching process took on a life of its own outside of the room. In Alan's case, and in many others, I believe that formal coaching processes encouraged an environment that made informal coaching possible, and even natural.

Fans

Last but not least, the sports analogy allows us to consider a third stakeholder group that is vested in a leader's journey of transformation: his or her fans. Fans can provide encouragement and inspiration for players during a game, in a playoff, and over the course of an entire season. This was certainly the case with the leaders in this book: most relied heavily on the support of their spouses, significant others, and friends in order to sustain their momentum and energy over time.

Tim's wife, Kristen, was a crucial source of support in his journey. As he recalls, "Kristen offered total acceptance of what I was trying to achieve, and really counseled patience and self-acceptance when times got tough."

I have also observed the reverse of this scenario several times, where a leader's partner is less than supportive. Obviously I don't want to mention any names here, but in one example, the husband did not appreciate his increasingly "enlightened" executive wife — my client — who, as a result of her leadership learning, was calmly refusing to engage in the aggressive interactions that had previously been commonplace in their relationship. Not only did this put stress on the marriage, it also created internal conflict for the leader, substantially slowing her progress.

We generally think of fans as passionately cheering their teams on, but true fans also will critique their favorite players when they feel their performance is substandard, and, if delivered in the right spirit, an apparently harsh critique can actually be very helpful. We saw in the Snowball chapter that the first measure of Mike's impact was so bad that he facetiously wondered out loud whether the printer had run out of blue ink. When he took his scary feedback home to show his wife, Kerstin, at that time a senior executive at Microsoft, he didn't get quite the sympathetic response he had hoped for: "She opened up the folder and she said, 'Blue is good, right?' I said, 'Yes, dear, that's right, blue is good.' My profile had almost zero blue. She looked at me and said, 'Actually, that feels about right. You can be a real [expletive] sometimes!' "

To this day, Mike tells this story to anyone who will listen. I believe it is because he is proud of the fact that he has a formidable partner in life, as well as the kind of relationship where they can be very honest with each other. He later told me that he received Kerstin's colorful language with a smile because he knew she had his best interests at heart — and also because she was right!

In my experience, moments like this can prove very powerful in a leader's transformation. When a spouse's feedback is consistent with the hard data, as well as the coach's and the team's view, leaders are quicker to accept their issues and more ready to make positive change. As a result, I now encourage all of the leaders I work with to engage their significant others early in the process of transformation. I encourage them to discuss their ambitions and to share their feedback very openly. For the majority who accept this advice, the moment they engage their significant other becomes a real point of acceleration on the journey.

Hunter S. Thompson got it right when he said, "He who is taught only by himself has a fool for a master." I strongly encourage any leader seeking to transform his or her leadership to involve all three stakeholder groups—external consultants (coaching staff), colleagues (teammates), and family (fans). Perhaps most importantly, what I have learned is that the coaching is most powerful when all three groups identify mutually beneficial outcomes from the leader's transformation—and create a trusting environment for that coaching to take place.

Now what?

If you're action oriented or ready to get some coaching, then I suggest you go to www.peterfuda.com and interact with the Coach audiovisual tools and exercises before coming back to read the next chapter. If you would prefer to keep reading, or you're not ready for any deep reflection yet, then here are a couple of simple next steps:

- Reflect on your previous coaching experiences and identify what you would do differently next time.
- Think about two to three peers with whom you would like to form a peer coaching team.
- Consider sharing your leadership goals with a loved one or friend and asking him or her to support you as you pursue those goals.

5

Mask

The metaphor of the Mask has two aspects: the concealment of perceived imperfections, and the adoption of an identity that is misaligned with a leader's authentic self, values, or aspirations.

MASKS HAVE BEEN PREVALENT across human cultures since the Stone Age and have been used in a variety of ways. In a theatrical context, masks are sometimes used to conceal a character's identity; at other times, they allow the actor to adopt a certain persona. It is these two notions of concealment and adoption of a persona that have enhanced my understanding of how a leader transforms.

For me, the metaphor of the Mask in a leadership context originated with Mike, the CEO of the IT multinational whom we've already met a couple of times in earlier chapters. You'll remember that Mike had a very strong personal burning platform to change: his feedback profile was so bad he worried the printer might have "run out of blue ink," and his wife, Kerstin, subsequently provided him with very honest and colorful (aka brutal) feedback of her own. I want to come back to Mike's story here because he achieved one of the biggest transformations of anybody I've ever worked with or encountered, and also because his story gets even more interesting and instructive when we consider it from the perspective of the Mask.

It was evident in the early days of my work with Mike that he was struggling in his new role. What was less clear to me until some years later was just how insecure Mike felt at that time. As I mentioned in the Fire chapter, on the surface Mike looked well equipped for the big job. Deep down, however, he was stretched to the breaking point in the leadership role. He wasn't particularly comfortable with customers, and he felt awkward around staff. So why had he gotten the job in the first place? To his way of thinking, he had gotten the job because his organization was a financially driven company and that was his area of expertise.

Adding to Mike's insecurity was the leadership experience of his father, who had been struck by a serious illness while he was the CEO and chairman of a large British manufacturing corporation. Rather than support him, upon his return to work, the company fired him. For Mike, this represented a double whammy to his sense of self-confidence; he had always wanted to follow in his father's footsteps, but he had witnessed how the CEO job could be taken away at any minute — even under the most dreadful of circumstances.

Mike struggled terribly under the pressure. He would alternate between being the aggressive guy who tried to control everything and the quiet guy in the corner who provided no leadership or direction: "I felt insecure in my promotion to such a big job so I tried to bluff my way through," Mike later confessed to me. "I thought, 'OK, I will be the tough guy. It is working for my boss; he is scaring the hell out of me.' But that didn't work, so I tried a different approach, 'I'll be the nice guy. Thank you for saying thank you! Oh, what a wonderful idea that is!' And that didn't work either. I was guessing and making it up as I went along. I was a bit of a fake."

Mike's vacillation spread confusion and anxiety — his team members were on tenterhooks, never quite sure which version of Mike was going to show up on any given day. In many cases, even *he* hadn't decided which Mike would show up until he entered the room! One thing was certain: nobody knew the real Mike back then, including Mike himself. As a result, everyone wasted time trying to second-guess him, and trust and rapport were low.

In my role as Mike's coach, I felt it was imperative to get this issue on the table, and I soon got my chance. You'll recall that Mike candidly accepted his data in front of his team even though it was a "horror story." This display of humility won him a great deal of support and admiration as he took his first tentative steps toward change. Now let me tell you about the aftermath of that moment, which his team did not see.

Mike arrived at my office for our scheduled one-on-one session just two weeks after the crushing feedback session with his team. As he sat down, I noticed the now-familiar red flush creeping up his neck. It became clear to me that he was really struggling to internalize the brutal feedback. I broke the ice by asking Mike how he was feeling about his feedback now that he had had some time to think about it. He avoided eye contact as he told me, somewhat sarcastically, that he was thinking of just "firing the bastards." This comment may have been dressed up as a joke, but there was an undertone that didn't sit right with me—it didn't feel authentic.

Mike's face was now completely flushed, but this was not the only sign that he was uncomfortable. There was a real incongruity between his words and his body language; his tone was humorous and ironic, but his posture screamed nervous, uncomfortable, and defensive.

In the split second that followed, I considered joining Mike in his nervous laughter but, mindful of what was at stake for him and his organization, I decided to take a direct approach. I told him that I did not believe he was genuine in his comment and that I wasn't buying the tough-guy façade he was trying to present. He hesitated for a moment, as if contemplating what to do next; I suspected that he was trying to work out whether to accept my feedback, or add me to the list of those he needed to fire. To my relief, he chose the former. "You're right," he admitted. "That felt awful. It's not me at all." And then, quite visibly, the tension appeared to leave his body. Even the flush began to fade.

In the two hours that followed, the tone of our conversation changed dramatically. He told me that he had been struggling to appear confident when all around him his world was in chaos. Even though deep down he knew that his team knew he was faking it, he was afraid to drop his mask for fear of looking weak. He told me that keeping up appearances was creating enormous internal conflict for him, and that he was relieved I had called him on it. He was ready to move on, but he wasn't sure how.

As the conversation progressed, we shifted our focus from his many problems to how we could leverage his strengths, namely resilience, humor, and a calm temperament. It became apparent to both of us that Mike needed to embrace these strengths and build his leadership identity around them.

Mike opened up on the vision he had for his leadership role, speaking passionately about the legacy that he wanted to leave of a growing organization that people were proud of. He also talked about the importance to him of family. He wanted to ensure that he remained a good husband to his wife, Kerstin, and a supportive father to his two teenage daughters. Mike spoke about his family with true sentiment.

We agreed that Mike shouldn't hide his human qualities from his colleagues at work. In effect, we could embrace his supposed flaws for advantage. His self-effacing, introverted style provided a real contrast to popular and heroic notions of leadership and distinguished him from his charismatic predecessor. We both felt that this very natural Everyman quality could be just the thing to reengage his disaffected staff and customers.

In the weeks and months that followed, Mike was surprised and delighted by the positive impact that just being himself—warts and all—had on his team. He found his groove with customers who appreciated his low-key approach, and staff loved how Mike was prepared to drop the polished presentations and just tell it like it was. As a result, Mike's annual town hall sessions with staff in thirty-two different locations across the country became legendary. And because his team no longer had to guess which Mike was going to show up, leadership meetings became much more focused and effective. Under his leadership, his organization went on to achieve five successive years of top- and bottom-line growth. What's more, Mike's happiness and confidence grew even faster than the numbers.

This story opened my eyes to just how prevalent masking is among leaders. Again and again we have encountered one of two distinct types of mask behavior in leaders. First, there is the Mask of concealment, where a leader hides imperfections and insecurities—this was the mask Mike had been wearing. Second, there is the Mask of persona, where a leader adopts an image he or she feels is necessary to be successful in their role. To explore the nuances of these two types of Mask, let me turn to two well-known examples from popular culture.

The Phantom of the Opera

To explore the Mask of concealment, I'm going to talk about Andrew Lloyd Webber's *The Phantom of the Opera*, the musical based on Gaston Leroux's classic novel of the same name. In book and musical, the Phantom wears a mask to conceal his physical imperfections. But while the Phantom presents a perfect, porcelain face to his audience, there is a certain irony at play here: it is starkly obvious that the mask is not his real face. The Phantom knows he is wearing a mask, the audience knows he is wearing a mask, and the Phantom knows that they know. Still, he prefers to maintain a façade rather than reveal the man behind the mask.

Just like the Phantom, Mike knew he was wearing a mask, his team knew he was wearing a mask, and he knew that his team knew — and yet there was an implicit understanding that no one was to talk about it. I have noticed this dynamic in many other leaders I have worked with. For example, Tim, the young advertising executive who helped to found Earth Hour, attempted to maintain the image of the golden boy while suffering a crisis of intense self-doubt. Clynton, the managing director of the international skin-care giant whom we met in the Snowball chapter, maintained an exterior of perfection despite feeling exhausted by the effort.

The common element in each of these leaders' stories is the desire to conceal imperfections and insecurities so that they would not be "found out." I now understand that the wearing of the Mask of concealment by a leader undermines trust and creates fear, doubt, and anxiety in others. Rather than take what the leader says at face value, subordinates will spend valuable time and energy trying to second-guess the leader's true intent. Inevitably, the energy spent trying to please the leader is energy that isn't spent on improving performance.

Stanley Ipkiss, aka "The Mask"

I have found evidence of masking in many leadership journeys, but not all of the leaders I have worked with were wearing the Phantom's mask in order to conceal their insecurities. Some of them deliberately put on a mask to project a particular persona. In this case, a leader isn't so much hiding as internalizing a persona to such a degree that they risk *becoming* it — at least at work.

To explore this second application of the Mask metaphor, let's turn to the 1994 Jim Carrey vehicle *The Mask.* Carrey's character, Stanley Ipkiss, is a shy man who discovers a mysterious green mask. Unbeknownst to Ipkiss, the mask channels Loki, the Norse trickster god. When Stanley brings the mask near his head, it melds with his face and transforms him into a confident, aggressive, and outgoing "superhero." With Loki's mask, Stanley becomes the man he thinks he needs to be in order to succeed in life.

In contrast to the Phantom, people perceive Stanley *as the mask* rather than as someone *hiding behind a mask.* Stanley eventually learns the hard way that the mask isn't all it's cracked up to be, as he inevitably scares off the love of his life and lands himself in jail. It's not until Stanley rids himself of his mask — which takes some doing — that he gets his happy ending.

This Mask of persona is something I have observed many times. Let's return to the story of Jim — not Jim Carrey this time, but the government leader we met in the Master Chef chapter. We saw how Jim masterfully navigated two of the biggest crises ever to hit Queensland: Cyclone Larry and the equine influenza. But if we wind back the clock to some fifteen years before these events, we encounter a Jim who wasn't quite the same enlightened leader.

Before his time in the Queensland state government, Jim worked in the public sector in the Australian state of Victoria. He had joined straight out of university and realized very quickly what he needed to "be" in order to get ahead in that organization. As Jim put it many years later: "We were like the Special Forces of the public sector. We were one-dimensional managers; command and control. I did very well under that structure."

Jim quickly developed a reputation as a tyrant — deliver the outcomes, or else get out of the way! By adopting this persona, Jim always got the top performance pay. But it came at great cost: his aggressive behavior increasingly damaged relationships and created enemies.

While his command-and-control persona had served him well early in his career, it did not work so well once he transferred into senior roles in Queensland. In fact, when Jim was an executive director in Queensland's Department of Primary Industries, his boss told him that he would never receive the top job unless he changed his very authoritarian behavior and became more collaborative.

This was a big moment for Jim because his ultimate aspiration was to become a director general—the government equivalent of a CEO. But his authoritarian Mask was attached very tightly indeed after fifteen years in the Victorian public sector, so it took a number of different influences and many years to chip away at it before Jim was able to remove it altogether.

In 1996, after an election, Jim was sidelined by the incoming government in Queensland. Subsequently, he underwent a period of serious reflection on his leadership, which led him to explore additional modes beyond his authoritarian persona. He undertook an experiential leadership development program, which helped to further loosen the Mask by opening him up to the "non-transactional" side of leadership. Perhaps more important, his teenage children started rejecting his bossy parenting style. Finally, Jim formed a close friendship with leadership guru Margaret (Meg) Wheatley, who encouraged him to get rid of his Mask by exploring the purpose and meaning of his work. So did his spiritual practice, which included adopting an ancient meditation technique, becoming a Knight of the Sovereign Military Order of Malta and Rhodes—an ancient Catholic order who work with the sick, poor, and disenfranchised around the world—and practicing an ancient form of Christianity within the Syro-Malabar Catholic Church.

When I became Jim's coach in 2003, I was able to draw these influences together by pointing out the incongruities between his spiritual beliefs and sense of purpose, and his authoritarian Mask. Just as Stanley Ipkiss eventually decides that his mask is not all it's cracked up to be, so too did Jim decide that his authoritarian persona was at odds with his deeply held values as a leader and a parent. Having shed the Mask, Jim went on to successfully lead four state government departments, and in 2009 was awarded an Order of Australia for services to government.

The burden of the Mask

While the initial motivations for wearing either type of Mask (that of concealment and that of persona) may be very different, the end result is often the same: the Mask becomes too heavy a burden to carry.

Brené Brown puts it beautifully in her book, *Daring Greatly*: "Masks and armor are perfect metaphors for how we protect ourselves from the discomfort of vulnerability. Masks make us feel safer even when they become suffocating. Armor makes us feel stronger even when we grow weary from dragging the extra weight around. The irony is that when we're standing across from someone who is hidden or shielded by masks and armor, we feel frustrated and disconnected."

This becomes apparent in both *The Phantom of the Op-*

era and *The Mask*, though only one story has a happy ending. The Phantom wears his mask until the very end, condemning himself to a lifetime of misery and loneliness. In contrast, once Stanley Ipkiss comes to the conclusion that wearing his mask exacts a heavy price, he goes to great lengths to rid himself of it. As Stanley connects with the best parts of himself—parts that were previously hidden—he gets the girl of his dreams.

In a business context, the wearing of a Mask creates poor outcomes in a leader's professional and private life, and often leads to inner conflict with the leader's deeply held values and aspirations. As a result, many leaders will reach a point where they want to "de-mask" as they realize it is no longer delivering success, and that not being able to show their true face has become a heavy psychological burden.

From our research, it is evident that there are several approaches that can enhance awareness of the Mask and, following from that, grow the ability to drop it. The first is through direct coaching interventions, such as the one I described above with Mike. Despite Mike's brave face and sense of humor during the team feedback session, he left the forum secretly wanting to "fire the bastards" who had painted a "horror story" in his data. He only dropped his Mask when I looked him in the eye and told him I wasn't buying the tough-guy routine. Of course, putting somebody on the spot in this manner is risky and requires the kind of strong foundation of trust and preparation that I described in the Coach chapter.

Another experience shared by many leaders in the book is

pressure from subordinates in a group forum. These forums were typically led by me or my colleagues to create a safe environment where the leader found it difficult to dismiss critical feedback for two reasons: they received similar feedback from multiple people and, somewhat ironically, they were being held accountable to a leadership agenda of their own making. The renowned management scholar Edgar Schein refers to this approach as "coercive persuasion." Schein also discusses the idea of using "grain against the grain" in order to induce guilt that encourages change. This involves pointing out incongruities between the Mask a leader wears and their deeply held values or aspirations. Becoming aware of such an inner contradiction is perhaps the most powerful factor in a leader's willingness to accept the failings of their Mask.

When I first met Anthony, he was the thirty-two-year-old managing director of an industry-leading advertising agency. His reputation preceded him; I knew that he was considered to be a rising star. Among other things, Anthony had created a beer commercial that became a YouTube sensation and had won more than thirty awards — including a Golden Lion at the Cannes Advertising Festival — catapulting him to superstar status.

Meeting him didn't disappoint, either. I found Anthony clever, funny, and charismatic. He was also clearly ambitious. Not long after our first meeting, he left the very comfortable world of advertising to take up a more challenging job as head of marketing for a huge beverages company.

It didn't take long for Anthony's anxiety to overtake his excitement. In this new corporate environment, he had no industry experience or established credibility. He became brash and argumentative, in effect adopting the persona of the know-it-all in order to prove himself in the new environment. He spent a lot of time managing up and not a lot of time focused on his team: "I ran a benevolent dictatorship. I was a nice guy who didn't really listen. A great meeting for me was one where I told you what to do, and you left feeling happy."

Anthony had gotten away with this type of leadership in the ad agency; people would follow him because he had earned his stripes and was considered something of a legend, even at his young age. But in his new role, his impact on colleagues was spotty. Some people liked him but saw him as an obstacle to getting things done, others went to great lengths to reveal the gaps in his knowledge and experience, and others still bowed to his perceived genius and just did what they were told.

Several factors led Anthony to question his overconfident, know-it-all Mask. He got very challenging leadership feedback that suggested he was encouraging his team to squash ideas and just follow the rules—something that was really at odds with his inherent values of creativity and innovation, and also a little ironic given his previous job and reputation. He was also struggling with real pressure on the home front. The arrival of his second child shone a bright light on just how poor his work–life balance had become and elicited feelings of guilt for not supporting his wife and baby daughter as well as he should.

As if all that wasn't enough, a new CEO took the helm and subsequently restructured the organization. From one moment to the next, Anthony found himself "surplus to requirements." He had been so focused on managing up that his direct reports could manage perfectly well without him! He was offered a "strategic role" in the new hierarchy but was smart enough to know what that meant: the writing was on the wall.

This was the first time in Anthony's career that he felt purposeless and lacking in confidence. He struggled to come to terms with how he had gone from young superstar to rock bottom so quickly. After much soul searching, Anthony came to the conclusion that all of his problems had exactly one thing in common: himself. He knew he had to change his ways in order to change his life.

Anthony resigned from his job in the beverages company to take on an even bigger executive position at a publicly listed clothing manufacturer and retailer. His new company had been a poster child for business success for decades but had lost its mojo in more recent times. Anthony realized that the new position gave him a second chance to start fresh, to be a better leader and a happier person, and he was determined to seize it. As we engaged in a transformation agenda together, his first commitment to me was to get rid of the know-it-all Mask and reconnect with his values of creativity and innovation, two things that the organization desperately needed.

In the personal realm, Anthony set very clear boundaries between his work and home life so that he could be fully present when he was with his family. He also started a disciplined exercise regime, something that had fallen away under the pressure of his previous role. In fact, he set himself the goal of one day following the Tour de France in an organized cycling tour, an ambition he realized in 2012.

Anthony became a valued member of the executive team and a revered leader in his business unit. The entrepreneurial spirit he brought to the business not only put them on an upward trajectory, but also meant that he had a queue of people wanting to work for him. In a retest of Anthony's leadership effectiveness six months into his new job, he scored dramatically better, shifting away from the negative behaviors he had been encouraging in his last role and toward the creativity, innovation, and teamwork he so deeply desired in himself and others. After only eighteen months at the company, and in stark contrast to his "surplus to requirements" experience in the previous organization, Anthony was asked by the board and his CEO to run the biggest business unit in the company.

Anthony's de-masking was certainly helped by the fact that he moved organizations; doing so provided the perfect opportunity for a fresh start. But as we saw in Mike and Jim's stories, it is not necessary to change organizations in order to drop your Mask.

What is common to all of the leaders I've worked with is that, once they dropped their Masks, they needed to rebuild their leadership identity in order to promote what Edgar Schein terms "psychological safety." In simple terms, they needed to transition from the Mask they have been wearing toward their more natural and authentic self.

I help leaders make this transition by exploring some Fire-inspired questions. For example, what do they want their lives to be about? What motivates them above and beyond making money? What do happiness and success look like for them? What are the most important roles in their lives, both professionally and personally?

Leaders also need to get clear on their most deeply held values and beliefs. In Anthony's case this was pretty straightforward: he was passionate about creativity and innovation as a force for good in organizations. Not only did these values come very naturally to him; he also had firsthand experience of what life looked like when he strayed from them. Mike was able to throw away his tough-guy Mask when we helped him connect to the more human side of himself that he displayed naturally with his family, and with his self-effacing sense of humor. Jim crafted a more purpose-driven leadership identity based on his spiritual practice and the influence of Meg Wheatley.

On occasion, leaders will "borrow" values and beliefs as a pathway to a more natural self. Mike borrowed one of my mantras — "Don't let perfect get in the way of better." This allowed him to feel safe as he built his leadership identity around his core values and his naturally humble, humorous, and self-effacing approach to life. As I said earlier, this mantra is one that I in turn borrowed from an early mentor in order to bridge the gap between my own streak of perfectionism and my more natural self.

The impact of de-masking

Taking off the Mask requires courage, but the rewards are exponential relative to the effort, both for the leader and for those they lead. Frances Hesselbein, one of the foremost contributors to leadership thinking, wrote: "Leadership is a matter of how to be, not how to do it. Only a person who is comfortable in his or her own skin, who has a strong set of values, who behaves consistently with those values, who demonstrates self-discipline, can begin to lead others."

Let's return to Christine, the CEO of the credit reporting and debt collection company whom we met in the Fire chapter. In the early days, Christine was under enormous pressure to lead the transformation of a "challenger" organization against huge established players, in the most macho of industries, with tens of millions of investment dollars at stake — not to mention her own reputation.

To tackle this enormous challenge, Christine put on a Mask of persona: toughness. At the time, this felt like a very logical thing to do, given that she had been conditioned by years of working in a male-dominated industry. She knew from experience it was survival of the fittest; the only way to succeed was to be highly competitive. So she needed to be seen as tough, in control, having all the answers. Whenever Christine's instincts for openness, warmth, and curiosity rose to the surface, she pushed them back down for fear of not being taken seriously.

The outcome was that Christine created a one-dimensional

work environment — have you delivered your numbers, yes or no? If yes, then you were a superstar. If no, then you had better raise your game quickly because after three strikes, you were out. There were no real conversations about the bigger picture, how to get better results through clever resourcing, increasing capabilities, or through innovation — it was all about "just get the results."

There was tension inside her organization, and that led to extreme tension and anxiety within Christine: "I felt like I was going through the motions because I had so much more to offer. I felt like I was cheating myself and the team. I wish I had listened to my instincts sooner, and operated in a more authentic way."

A real turning point for Christine was when she began employing really smart executives — people she considered smarter than herself. They were harder to fool, but they also brought out more of Christine's natural curiosity and openness. It led to a shift in mindset for Christine. Previously she had felt that everyone was there to execute her plan. Now, with the Mask of toughness and control coming off, her eyes were opening to the power of what they could achieve together.

"I became more comfortable, relaxed, and happier," Christine later told me. "We lost a lot of the unnecessary formality in our interactions and began to have very rich conversations. I've learned that authenticity comes from confidence, and confidence comes from taking risks. The challenge is that you can't take risks unless you're prepared to be vulnerable — it's actually a sign of strength."

The team came out of Christine's shadow. They became more

confident, individually and collectively. And together, they shot the lights out, achieving a tenfold increase in revenue. They took on the industry big boys and came out on the other end as the recognized benchmark in the industry for excellence and performance.

Christine is now an independent director on several boards, and president of Chief Executive Women, a think tank and networking organization for top female CEOs. Recently, I asked Christine what advice, based on her own experiences, she gives today to young female executives on the way up. Her response was less about gender, and more about dropping the Mask: "I place no value on the literature talking about how to succeed as a woman in business. It's too binary. One school says 'be tough,' and the other one says 'be a nurturer.' It's bloody confusing and completely unhelpful. What about 'just be yourself'?"

Mahatma Gandhi once said: "Happiness is when what you think, what you say, and what you do are in harmony." The Mask metaphor is essentially about finding this level of congruence.

As one of our research subjects put it: "The power this congruence unleashes is practically atomic in scale. You get more done, you build more trust, your interactions with people become more enriching, you feel more fulfilled, and on it goes."

Now what?

If you're action oriented or ready to take off your Mask, then I suggest you go to www.peterfuda.com and interact with the

Mask audiovisual tools and exercises before coming back to read the next chapter. If you would prefer to keep reading, or you're not ready for any deep reflection yet, then here are a couple of simple next steps:

- Consider what imperfections you might be concealing, or what persona(s) you adopt to be "successful."
- Reflect on whether these masks conflict with your values and aspirations, and the cost to you of that conflict.
- Think about how you could bring more of your authentic self to work.

6

Movie

The Movie metaphor involves processes for increasing self-awareness and reflection that allow leaders to first "edit" their performance, and then direct a "movie" that exemplifies their leadership vision.

S HAKESPEARE GAVE US the metaphor of life as a stage in Jaques's famous monologue in *As You Like It*, according to which "all the men and women [are] merely players." Ever since, sociologists and philosophers alike have been using this metaphor in statements such as "society is a theater and all acts are performances," and that each of us seeks to "manage" the impressions we make on others. In the Mask chapter, we explored the potential downside of impression management, and made a case in favor of moving toward a more authentic self. But as

I hope I made clear earlier in this book, articulating a vision is one thing; having the capacity to bring that vision to life is another. To make this transition, we'll move beyond the notion of the stage and unfold the metaphor of Movie.

The Movie metaphor allows us to explore how leaders can enhance their reflective practices and their self-awareness, and in doing so create an impact that is in line with their leadership vision. There are three applications of the Movie metaphor that have enhanced my understanding of leadership transformation: acting in a repetitive movie; viewing footage in the editing suite; and finally, directing your own movie.

To explore these three aspects of the metaphor, I return to Sylvia, the Australian managing director of the leading American fast-moving consumer goods company whom we met in the Snowball chapter. Having told the story of how Sylvia unlocked increasing levels of accountability and performance in her executive team and senior managers, I'll now dive more deeply into Sylvia's personal story, particularly regarding how she leveraged increasing levels of self-awareness and reflection to transform her leadership and her organization. Sylvia's background provides us with insight into the nature of these challenges, so let's start there.

Sylvia grew up in the idyllic setting of Rotorua, one of the most beautiful and picturesque towns in New Zealand, famous for its great lakes and bubbling mud pools, as well as its vibrant and friendly culture and people. The eldest of three girls, Sylvia is the first to tell you that she was introverted and quiet compared to her more outgoing sisters. When she was seven, she declared that her life's mission was to be a doctor, but after her first year of pre-med, her life took a different turn. She decided medicine wasn't her calling after all.

Young and unsure about just what her purpose was, Sylvia fell into sales, a job that seemed attractive to her at the time primarily because of the promise of a company car. It was this small carrot that changed the course of Sylvia's life. Despite her introversion, Sylvia was very good at sales thanks to her natural warmth and genuine passion for the company's products, philosophies, and values. It wasn't long before she was promoted up the ranks: first in sales, then human resources — including six years in the United States — until eventually she became the managing director for New Zealand. After leading a turnaround in the New Zealand business, Sylvia was promoted across the Tasman Sea to lead the Australian organization — which she found equal parts exciting and daunting.

The new role had five times the staff and six times the revenue. And it attracted a lot of attention globally because it made up roughly half the corporation's revenue and profit in the Asia-Pacific region and was a significant supply unit to other markets in the region as well. If Australia sneezed, Asia got the flu and the global business caught a cold. Sylvia's company was still the market leader but had been consistently losing small amounts of market share for ten consecutive years as aggressive competitors chipped away at them. Sylvia's job was to arrest this decline and reassert the company's leadership. This meant leading a turnaround in the company culture—from passive and reactive to innovative and proactive. It was similar to the transformation she had led in New Zealand, but on a much greater scale.

On a personal level, Sylvia was conflicted; accepting the new role meant leaving her two adult children in New Zealand. One was in the last year of high school, and the other was struggling with Asperger's syndrome and the adjustment to university life.

It came as a relief, at least initially, that her new team seemed to respond well to her open and inclusive style—a style that was quite different from that of her predecessor. As Sylvia got a better handle on her new work environment, however, her impression changed. People seemed to talk a good game and were verbally supportive of the cultural shifts Sylvia was driving, but she seemed to be pushing against an undercurrent of passive resistance: "In one executive meeting I was getting really frustrated with one of our leaders. He was really pushing my buttons—not purposefully—but he seemed to be giving every excuse under the sun about why sales were down. And it drives me mad when people make excuses rather than take responsibility for their results. And so I smiled through gritted teeth, took a deep breath, and gave him some suggestions for how to improve his results. My intent was good, but my body language was telegraphing to everybody that I'm really pissed off. People said to me after this meeting that it was the scariest thing they'd ever seen in their life—and here I was really proud of myself for not losing my cool!"

For Sylvia, her typical day meant fighting this passive undercurrent as she tried to implement positive change in the organization. It was incredibly draining—physically, mentally, and emotionally. Making progress was much harder than what Sylvia had originally anticipated, and certainly slower than the turnaround she'd led in New Zealand. In fact, a few months into her new position, Sylvia was starting to doubt that she was right for the job.

About three months after we began our partnership, Sylvia and I had a one-on-one coaching session during which we tried to make sense of incidents such as the one above. I'd seen the frustration bubble up inside her; her face would redden, and she would grip the table as she described the incidents that so infuriated her. But it wasn't until Sylvia stepped back and reflected on the issues driving her frustration that she realized how much of her misery was self-inflicted. She set very high, almost impossible standards and expectations for herself and for others. When she applied these standards to the rest of the world, she inevitably ended up frustrated. And when she got frustrated, she would unleash a formidable temper that became known among her team as the "Sylvia spike," after which no constructive resolution to an issue was possible. I remember Sylvia's face when this penny dropped and she realized that she had been exacerbating her own problems—she initially looked stunned, and then she flashed me a wry smile as if to say, "How could I have been so stupid?"

A distinction that really resonated with Sylvia was what I call a shift from judging to perceiving. It's been my observation over the years that when leaders are unhappy or frustrated, it is often because they are negatively judging people, circumstances, and events too frequently and too quickly. They lose their sense of objectivity and their ability to empathize, creating a downward spiral of frustration, or worse, and wasting enormous amounts of time and energy. The shift to perceiving means hitting the pause button and asking, "What else could be going on here?" It invites exploration and alternative meanings that encourage the leader to remain calm and expand their choices. It also allows the leader to step out of the Movie, to analyze it from a more detached perspective, and effectively contemplate their role in the unfolding issue.

"I was working *really* hard and I was disappointed and frustrated *all* the time about *everything,*" Sylvia later told me. "And that had a terrible impact on others. When I got the difference between judgment and perception it all made sense, and I was able to leave that behind very quickly. In every meeting I have, I write that phrase at the top of my page—'from judging to perceiving.'"

The shift from judgment to perception is deceptively simple, but it was massive to Sylvia. It allowed her to enhance her capacity for deep self-reflection, and made it easier for others to give her feedback. In the past, Sylvia had been quite disciplined about getting feedback, but her low frustration threshold meant that her team was afraid to stick their necks out. So my colleague Martin and I instituted regular feedback forums for Sylvia and her executive team to help everybody step out of their

Movie in order to analyze the footage and their behavior objectively. You could say that these forums developed into a healthy obsession, as Sylvia explains: "My team talks about feedback fatigue because whenever we have a meeting, we always take time to reflect on our behaviors and the impact we're having. So that's happening all the time now."

Sylvia's team quickly responded to her new sense of calm and openness. Once they understood that Sylvia genuinely wanted feedback, they started giving it to her more often and in formal and informal settings. The increasing levels of trust and openness also allowed us to up the ante. One structured reflection session that we ran with Sylvia's executive team was what we affectionately call speed-dating. We gave people a week to prepare a list of what they would like each of their colleagues to start doing, stop doing, and continue doing, and then gave them twenty minutes with each one — ten minutes giving feedback and ten minutes receiving feedback — before ringing the bell and moving them on to the next person. The process was a revelation for Sylvia: "[Speed-dating] was really valuable to get some affirmation, and then some stuff to improve. But the interesting thing was, I got a lot of 'stop doing this' and when I probed more deeply, it was 'well, yeah, you haven't done it for three months but we still don't want you to forget to stop doing it.' So it was more reinforcement of the changes that I had been making, and that was really confidence-building."

With all of this disciplined, reflective practice, over time Sylvia became very adept at calming her frustration before it bubbled over. In fact, she learned to change her behavior in the moment, even with one executive who'd been the cause of many frustrations for her. In a recent meeting, my colleague Martin observed the whole executive team become frustrated with his behavior; everyone, that is, except Sylvia. Rather than get trapped in a downward spiral, Sylvia calmly redirected the conversation to the agreed next steps. After the meeting, one team member told Sylvia that she "deserved a medal for her composure."

Sylvia's story illustrates the three applications of the Movie metaphor that help us enhance our understanding of leadership transformation. First, there is the notion of being trapped in a repetitive loop, doing the same thing day in and day out and getting the same poor results. Second, there is stepping out of the Movie and viewing the footage objectively in what I call the editing suite. Finally, there is the ability—earned over time and with lots of practice—to effectively direct your own Movie in accordance with your leadership vision, in real time.

Groundhog Day

Even though all of the leaders I have worked with are unique, the common thread for most is that at the outset of their leadership journeys, they felt as though they were trapped in a repeating scenario—just like Phil Connors, the Pittsburgh TV weatherman played by Bill Murray in Harold Ramis's classic *Groundhog Day* (1993). At six o'clock every morning, Connors wakes up to Sonny and Cher's "I Got You Babe" playing on the radio, and to the dreaded realization that he is doomed to repeat the same day over and over again. He is trapped in Groundhog Day.

In a similar fashion, many of the business leaders I've worked with would wake up and relive a similar reality, day after day after day. One of them would wake up dreading the seemingly endless queue of subordinates lining up at his door, looking for direction. Another's Groundhog Day revolved around adjudicating the conflict among her executive team members. Yet another's involved trying to muscle his way out of a dire financial situation. And another would climb out of bed with the horrible feeling that, no matter what she tried, the day would be a struggle. Like Bill Murray's character, these leaders did not comprehend that they were perpetuating their Groundhog Day through their own actions and the impact these actions had on others. This was because they lacked the time, the space, and the reflective capabilities to plot a way out.

In the Fire chapter, we met Alan, the CEO of a subsidiary of a German multinational pharmaceutical and chemical company. Alan felt that he had inherited something of a "Prussian empire" because of the autocratic management style of his predecessor, the command-and-control tendencies of headquarters, and the staff disengagement that had resulted from this approach to leadership.

Alan was determined to lead differently—to be much more engaging, inclusive, and constructive—but he soon found himself trapped in his very own Groundhog Day. Alan's daily battle involved trying to wrestle some control over his organization from a highly centralized and directional head office and protecting his staff from "unreasonable global demands." It involved seeking recognition from his bosses for a job well done, but never getting it. As a result, Alan experienced high levels of stress, anger, and fatigue, and a sense of frustration — it seemed like he was powerless to make the positive changes he so desperately wanted to make. Alan's days usually ended with late-night phone arguments with his international colleagues rather than with his reading bedtime stories to his young daughter.

But there is more to this story. Alan was not just a victim of the role — he had become very adept at playing the victim. Over his thirty-year career, Alan had internalized the leadership ideals of head office to such an extent that he had the same negative impact on his own staff. Of course, at first he couldn't see this because he was so consumed by his Groundhog Day routine and the victim mentality that he had adopted to cope.

In the movie, Phil Connors becomes aware that he is somehow trapped in a seemingly endless loop, but he does not realize for some time that it's his behavior and actions that are keeping him there. It is only when, inspired by his love interest, Rita, played by Andie MacDowell, he reflects on his behavior that he finds a way to move beyond Groundhog Day. Similarly, in the early stages of their journeys, Alan and the other leaders in this book did not fully comprehend that they were perpetuating their misery through their own actions. And even as they did begin to realize that they were trapped in Groundhog Day, they lacked the time and space to reflect on how they could get out of it. Ironically, it is the very act of disciplined reflection that allows leaders to understand how they are reinforcing the repetitive loop they're trapped in, and eventually to break out of it. This leads me to the second application of the Movie metaphor, the concept of the editing suite.

The editing suite

In the editing suite, the raw footage of a film is reviewed to determine its value to the movie as a whole. Following this review, changes are made: bits that confuse the plot or that might distract the audience are edited out; scenes are rearranged; the best cut of any given scene is selected. Similarly, leaders can use the editing suite to reflect on their performance and "edit" their future behavior for maximum impact.

It was actually Alan who gave me the idea for the editing suite metaphor: "The biggest thing on this journey is, you move from not knowing to knowing about yourself, and it's the realization on that journey that if you want change, the first thing that's got to change is you. You've got to have a damn hard look at yourself. Standing outside of yourself and looking at yourself as though you are seeing yourself replayed on video is very powerful."

The first time Alan and I entered the editing suite together was for a very confrontational conversation at the beginning of

his leadership journey. As I mentioned in "Read This First" at
the start of this book, when I ask leaders to fill in the Leader-
ship/Impact survey describing their vision for their leadership,
they almost always have a very "constructive" ideal. That is, they
want to motivate people to achieve goals, build quality relationships, and the like. Unfortunately, Alan's ideal did not exactly
conform to this theory. He had said that he wanted these things,
but his survey results revealed that he also wanted people in his
organization to compete with one another, oppose the ideas of
others, and build up their power base. And it wasn't just a little of these aggressive behaviors — Alan wanted them up around
the ninetieth percentile!

Over the years, Alan and I have spoken many times about
where this atypical ideal came from, and we have come to the
conclusion that he was mirroring the authority figures in his
life. In any case, Alan came to realize that he was not just a victim of a very autocratic culture at corporate HQ; he was perpetuating it in his organization to the point where he had created
his very own Groundhog Day: "I've always had a problem with
the head office culture of banging the table and using power-ori-
ented stuff; however, I grew up in that culture, so I had started
to internalize it. I have to say now when I look back to reflect on
it, I'm appalled by it."

This first trip to the editing suite brought to the surface a set
of beliefs that Alan was harboring at a subconscious level; they
had previously not been accessible to him in a conscious way.
Now that these beliefs had surfaced via the survey results, he

was able to assess them in a more rational way and let go of the ones that were not serving him well. We subsequently brought his executive team into the editing suite as well, in the form of team workshops, to help Alan identify his blind spots—with great effect. He later recalled one memorable example: "When I first got my survey results and I looked at my very high competitive score, I couldn't see it. Then a colleague gave the example of a meeting where someone came in late and I used the famous Billy Connolly line [delivered when audience members arrived late to the comedian's stand-up act], 'You haven't missed anything, I was only killing time until you got here.' I had actually thought that was really funny until I began to understand the impact on that individual—making her feel two feet tall. I later found out that she was late because of a serious personal problem."

Alan and I share a penchant for spoiling a good walk in the sunshine with a futile pursuit called golf—especially the way we play it. A couple of weeks after that very first trip into the editing suite, we found ourselves hacking our way around a very picturesque course when the conversation turned to the origin of Alan's very aggressive vision for his leadership. His raw honesty and insight stopped me dead in my tracks: "I felt like nothing I did was ever good enough for my dad. I think getting my Ph.D. at twenty-three was about proving that I was something to him. My push to advance up the corporate ladder was probably about the same thing: proving I was good enough. My father was a real bully, physically and emotionally. What do you do as a five-year-old boy when your mother is being beaten in the next room? I could never compete with him physically so I chose other paths to feel good about myself. My brother used to say, 'I bet you will be relieved when he dies.' Actually it left a huge hole."

It was very hard to make small talk on the golf course after that revelation. In fact, we spent most of the afternoon in the clubhouse in a very deep conversation about how our upbringing affects us later in life. Alan did most of the talking while I did most of the listening, partly because Alan just needed a friendly ear but also because I did not know what to say. My coaching experience at that point was pretty shallow and I did not want to trivialize Alan's insight. What I was able to help Alan connect in his mind was that the leaders who so infuriated him in headquarters were also the products of their experiences, just like he was. I offered him the notion that people do the best they can with what they know. Once Alan accepted this notion, he was better able to let go of the victim mentality, and the countless conspiracy theories that occupied his thinking, and this became a guidepost for us moving forward.

After that conversation on the golf course, Alan committed to his leadership journey with renewed vigor. The energy that he had been injecting into changing headquarters was now focused inward on changing himself. And one thing I learned about Alan very early on was that once he set his mind to something, he was relentless in his pursuit of it.

Not surprisingly, as Alan stepped out of his personal Groundhog Day, his outcomes changed quite dramatically. His stress and tension went down almost as fast as the work–life balance in his life increased. At work, staff engagement increased to unprecedented levels, and the company exceeded its financial targets for three consecutive years. In fact, the transformation story was so powerful that Alan became an in-demand keynote speaker and media personality. At age fifty-four, he made a graceful exit from the company he had served for thirty years to follow his passion and start a new career — as a consultant and coach in leadership transformation.

Our concept of the editing suite can be compared to organizational theorist Donald Schön's notion of "reflection-on-action." As the phrase suggests, reflection-on-action occurs after a given situation has unfolded, when the central character reflects on the situation alone or in conversation with others. These reflections then inform future situations, where they offer more choices or ideas to draw upon in a given moment. Since Alan inspired me to come up with the Movie metaphor, I have become a lot more literal and purposeful in my use of it; in particular, I'm quite deliberate in my approach to the editing suite.

Based on what I've learned from Alan and other leaders, I now use a very structured approach to reflection-on-action in my one-on-one coaching. These sessions happen within the context of the leader's most important goals — goals that we agree on together up front and revise at regular intervals. In a sense, these goals are the scenes in the Movie we want to make. As we review each goal, I ask, "How are you tracking against this goal, and why?" When the leader reveals they are off-track, it presents an opportunity to bring to the surface strategies or habits that are ineffective and self-defeating. If the leader reveals they are on-track, it presents an opportunity to reinforce strategies that work. At the end of these sessions, we will almost always have homed in on one or two patterns—helpful or unhelpful—that become the focus for the next few weeks.

Another way I take leaders into the editing suite is somewhat opportunistic—for example, immediately following a team workshop. These private conversations between me and the leader work on the premise that movies are best discussed and debated while they are still fresh in your mind. I ask the respective leader to critique the Movie that has just taken place through a fairly standard series of questions including: How effective was the session? How effective was your impact? What did you do well? What would you do differently next time?

Once the leader has given me his or her answers, I provide my own reflections on the same questions, emphasizing any points of difference. The idea behind this process is to arrive at a picture of two or three simple things that will allow the leader to move forward. The more we practice this reflective process, the more the leaders become proficient at seeing their Movie from multiple vantage points. These simple practices can dramatically increase a leader's effectiveness, so I encourage you to consider how you could integrate them into your workday.

My colleagues and I have also found it useful to bring a leader's whole team into the editing suite at least once a quarter to reflect on their progress against their leadership action plans, to deliver a structured update to the group, and to receive peer feedback and reflection on their progress. We have found that compelling leaders to reflect publicly on their journey can solicit new insights from colleagues, and has the added benefit of encouraging high levels of accountability.

All of these mechanisms help to build the necessary muscles for reflection and increased self-awareness, allowing leaders to eventually take themselves into the editing suite without our involvement. The more they reflect, the better results they get, the more they value it, and, consequently, the more they do it. Another example of the Snowball effect in action.

Some leaders can even reach a high enough level of reflective capability that they are able to pause their Movie, take themselves to a quiet place where they can review the footage, and make better choices in real time.

Geoff was a young, fast-moving consumer-goods executive. His first job out of university was with a leading multinational beverages company where he got a "stellar corporate education." He seemed to have a natural talent for improving the customer experience, which helped to propel him up the management ranks. This was underpinned by a philosophy from his background in sports of the need to first be a good follower in order to be a good leader. After ten years there, he sought a new challenge and landed himself a senior category management role in a division of a publicly listed food company. With the subsequent privatization of the business, Geoff was promoted to the managing director role for the newly created branded food division of the company at just thirty-three years old.

Geoff found himself in a far more chaotic environment than he had ever experienced before. He was responsible for many huge and fast-moving consumer brands. At the same time, he was encouraged by the new owner to drive big changes; specifically, he was urged to shift the business from looking inward to focusing on the customer. Those early years felt like a lifetime to Geoff. He loved his work but he was moving at a sprinter's pace all day long, trying to do it all. His Groundhog Day was a frantic rush in which he was completely consumed by the task at hand.

Geoff's energy and commercial acumen led to great success for his division over a period of six years — three under private ownership and three back in the publicly listed environment; the division's revenue, profit, and head count all doubled. Toward the end of this period, however, it became clear to Geoff and his CFO that they had really pushed the business as far as they could. Growth had begun to slow and the old tricks weren't working anymore. Geoff decided that in order to unlock the next level of growth, he needed to invest in his leadership team and his next level of twenty senior managers. Until that point, the business had been led very tightly by Geoff and his CFO. In order to keep growing, they needed to step back and allow the rest of the leadership group to step up.

Around this time, Geoff heard me speak at a business networking dinner and sought me out after the session. He said that my seven metaphors really resonated with him—he identified with the notion of the Movie, and *Groundhog Day* in particular. Geoff had always considered himself a very self-reflective kind of guy, but the truth was, under the immense pressure of his role, like Sylvia, Alan, and the other CEOs in this book, he lacked the time, space, and mechanisms to see how he was perpetuating his own problems. And so, a few weeks after we first met, our companies began working together on a transformation agenda.

The framework for our engagement called for executive team meetings every two months, and a senior leaders' forum with the executive team and the next level of twenty senior managers every quarter. At a basic level, these sessions forced the top thirty leaders in the business to reflect on what was working, what was not, and what they would do differently in the following months to increase their effectiveness—individually and collectively. Given the frantic nature of their environment to that point, Geoff and his team really enjoyed the opportunity to take some time out from their repetitive Movie and reflect on how they could do the necessary editing work on it.

Geoff later summed up the impact of this initial phase of the transformation process: "One of the biggest benefits of this work was having language and processes that we could use in meetings. For example, where we spend the first fifty minutes of a conversation in the meeting and then we spend ten minutes at the end reflecting on the meeting. That's where we got all the richness. It wasn't me trying to psychoanalyze them, it was their opportunity to make me better, and my opportunity to do the same for them. We were a group of people who didn't know what we didn't know, so having simple ways for us to articulate issues in a reflective and unemotional way worked brilliantly for us."

In the process of disciplined self-reflection, Geoff came to the key insight that he was not giving his team the space to be successful. He realized that it was OK to not be fixing things all the time, to step back and observe what was going on. Soon, Geoff started taking himself into the editing suite: "I deliberately made an effort to slow down and step out. I can be impatient. If I want something done, I will ask you over and over and over again, 'Is it done, is it done, is it done?' Once is OK, but I was relentless."

Geoff developed a novel way to break free from his Groundhog Day tendencies — he called it "hitting the pause button." Whenever Geoff found himself dominating an interaction with his team, he would literally pause the meeting and take himself out. He'd explain why he was leaving, and create a setting for his direct reports to reach a decision in his absence. This approach, along with the more typical reflection processes I have talked about in this chapter, worked really well for Geoff. They helped him to slow down long enough to consider his actions, understand his choices, and better access all of the experiences and insights that had gotten him the job in the first place.

Over time, Geoff became calmer, more confident, and far more effective in his role. The feedback from his team — both formal and anecdotal — confirmed his increasing effectiveness. They relished the space that Geoff now gave them and loved the collective approach to leadership, an approach that enabled the team to reignite the business's growth trajectory in the years following.

Despite all of Geoff's success, he is aware that he still has to be very vigilant with his reflective processes: "I am getting better and better at recognizing those moments where I need to hit the pause button and walk away and stop and reflect. But recognizing and changing it in the moment is hard. I am getting better, but I'm not there yet."

In my experience, Geoff's ongoing challenge is quite common. I have many case studies of successful transformation, but the ability to reflect in the moment takes considerable time and practice for most people. This naturally leads me to the third application of the Movie metaphor.

Directing the Movie

As leaders' reflective practices are honed into a habit by repeated visits to the editing suite, they become more and more proficient at the third element of the Movie metaphor: directing their own Movies — in real time. The process of film directing involves articulating and then adhering to the overall vision for the movie. It is all about planning the audience's experience. And although directors will often spend a lot of time in the editing suite, analyzing and making sense of the footage, much of their direction occurs on the set, in real time, where they must make key decisions as the action is unfolding, thinking on their feet and making adjustments as they go.

This type of reflective processing is what Donald Schön calls "reflection-in-action" as opposed to "reflection-on-action." It involves looking to our past experiences, connecting with our emotions, and challenging our habits and behaviors—and being able to do all of this in the moment. In my experience, this heightened level of reflective capability emerges later in a leader's journey, and only after they have systematically practiced reflection-on-action for some time.

The ability to reflect in action means slowing the Movie down. As a leader effectively expands the space between a given stimulus and response, they are better able to draw upon their repertoire of tools and strategies and direct a Movie that is more aligned with their leadership vision. To explore this third and arguably most advanced aspect of the Movie metaphor, let's return to Clynton, the managing director of the German skincare giant we met in the Snowball chapter. Clynton's story is one of the longest case studies we were able to conduct over the course of our research and consulting practice—it covers some eight years—so we can clearly see the progression from reflection-on-action to reflection-in-action.

Clynton had worked his way up from a junior marketing role and, some nine years later, had become the youngest country manager in the global corporation. Clynton knew his business backward and forward, and this made him want to solve everyone's problems. He felt he was being really efficient by finishing people's sentences! As a result of his behavior, over time Clynton's team came to rely on him for all important decisions, exhausting him in the process. Clynton's Groundhog Day—having to solve problems everywhere, all the time—prevented him from putting his attention where it needed to be: on creating a future for his organization.

In the first year of our work together, my colleague Leanne brought Clynton and his executive team together every single month, and the top sixty managers every quarter, to reflect on their progress to date and plan the next steps in their journey. Clynton and I met one-on-one every month to track his progress, but he also met monthly with Leanne to prepare for the important meetings in his calendar over the next month, including town halls, customer interactions, and executive team one-on-ones. These meetings, where Clynton and Leanne would plan out the impact he wanted to have, proved invaluable because they allowed him not only to reflect backward, but also to reflect forward. "Those meetings forced me to reflect and say, 'This would have been my normal approach, so I am actually going to construct my approach differently to get the outcome that I want.'"

More and more, Clynton began to catch himself in moments when he was not having the impact he wanted, and this was not just reserved for what was coming out of his mouth; he realized his body language could undermine his impact, too.

"I desperately wanted more exchange of ideas from the people who worked for me," he recalled later. "But I also realized my nonverbal cues had been letting me down. I remember sitting in a meeting, watching people watch me, and they were just looking for clues. And as soon as I rolled my eyes, that was it. People did not volunteer ideas any further."

One technique in particular really helped Clynton improve his impact: just being quiet once in a while. (Which for Clynton was quite a bit more difficult than it sounds.) His executive team had become so conditioned to Clynton articulating his ideas first that they had lost the habit of taking initiative and thinking for themselves. This ended up dragging Clynton into the business's day-to-day operations. His use of silence enabled him to become more mindful of his impact and to create space for others to fill. Initially, his team found the silence difficult, but then they started to fill the voids with good ideas. And while they may not have solved each problem exactly as Clynton would have, the business still got great outcomes. Only now, his team members owned the outcomes and experienced the satisfaction and confidence that comes with solving your own problems: "I remember on one occasion a direct report of mine, one who is also very prone to putting her ideas up front, actually saying to me, 'Wow, that was a great use of silence. You just let me fill in the blanks. And I know it took me a while, but I feel really committed to this solution now. You know what? I'm going to use that technique with my people.'"

Eventually, Clynton became adept at reflection-in-action; that is, thinking on his feet and modifying his behavior in the moment. In one very memorable example, he caught himself encouraging competitive behavior between his head of sales and head of marketing: "The old me would have been comfortable believing that I was actually driving them to a better outcome, rather than that I was actually damaging their relationship and potentially driving internal competition right through the organization. I caught myself and corrected the behavior. Both of them were quite amazed that I did that and it became a powerful lesson for me and for the whole team, which people still talk about today, years later."

Clynton's reflective practices were effectively enabling him to slow down his Movie, creating the time and space to choose a better response while a situation was still unfolding. Of course, the ability to slow down and experiment with a different behavior in real time does not necessarily guarantee a successful outcome. Rather, it helps leaders make more conscious and informed choices, to draw upon past experience, and to access their repertoire of leadership tools and strategies — under pressure.

Clynton reached a place where he could reflect-in-action through much disciplined practice, being mindful of his body language, and his clever use of silence. But there are other techniques I have used personally, and that I encourage other leaders to use, in order to direct their Movie in the moment on a consistent basis.

The benefits of meditation to our physical, mental, and emotional health are now widely accepted, but I've also found it a great tool for slowing down the Movie, particularly with A-type personalities like yours truly. In the process of trying to meditate, you become very conscious of the cacophony of voices in your head (or maybe that's just me). As I have gotten better and better at quieting those voices in my brief morning practice, I have found that I'm able to be much more present during the day, particularly under pressure, when I really need access to all of my resources and experience. It's like building up a bank of deposits that I can draw upon at key moments during the day. Most of the leaders whom I've encouraged to develop a meditation practice — even if it's just the simple action of closing their eyes and breathing deeply for ten minutes a day — have found it very helpful in increasing their mindfulness and presence at work.

The other technique I have found useful is applying the Socratic method, otherwise known as open-ended questions — that is, questions beginning with who, what, when, where, how, and why. Under pressure, most of us will respond to a question, comment, or suggestion by telling the other party what we think. Our goal may be to solve an issue quickly, but often we are perpetuating our Groundhog Day — never mind that we are probably encouraging dependent behavior in the other party. Asking an open-ended question not only encourages the other party to think, it gives us time to explore a whole range of potential alternatives. It helps us create the space to direct a better Movie.

Reflection-in-action is a real sweet spot, and in my experience, leaders who can direct their own Movie in real time are extremely effective. But the key insight I want you to take away from this chapter is the importance of the editing suite or reflection-on-action; big gains can be made here, and this process underlies any serious and lasting change. Regular trips to the editing suite build the reflective muscle that allows leaders to transform.

The idea of disciplined reflection is so pervasive in leadership literature that it could be almost considered a truism. For Alan, the notion stretched all the way back to his childhood: "My mum used to say all the time in her wonderful Manchester slang, 'I wish the Lord the gift he gives us, to see ourselves as others see us.' I used to think, 'Yeah, Mum, whatever.' Turns out she was spot on!"

In practice, however, it rarely happens. Leaders are often so consumed fighting fires that they lack the time, space, and practice to get out of their personal Groundhog Day. But, as I hope the stories in this chapter have demonstrated, the investment is well and truly worth it — and leadership transformation simply doesn't happen without it.

Now what?

If you're action oriented or ready to direct a better Movie, then I suggest you go to www.peterfuda.com and interact with the Movie audiovisual tools and exercises before coming back to read the next chapter. If you would prefer to keep reading, or you're not ready for any deep reflection yet, then here are a couple of simple next steps:

- Consider the ways in which your life resembles *Groundhog Day*, and how you might be perpetuating this reality.
- Reflect on how often you operate from a place of judgment as opposed to perception.
- Think about who could help you reflect-on-action.

7

Russian Dolls

The Russian Dolls metaphor describes a complementary set of journeys that interact with a leader's personal journey, thereby increasing levels of effectiveness.

R USSIAN NESTING DOLLS, also known as *matryoshka* dolls, are typically made of wood and contain three to eight identically shaped dolls nested neatly inside one another. When you pull one doll apart, another one, slightly smaller, sits inside. Each doll in a set typically resembles the others, but may bear a unique image or pattern. While the traditional appearance of a Russian doll is a peasant woman, some of the most prized collectibles do not show a figure or face at all. Rather, they tell a story through different images painted on each doll in the set.

Russian dolls have inspired a design principle known as the "matryoshka principle," representing an object-within-object relationship similar to the onion metaphor where one layer is peeled back to reveal another layer underneath. In our context, the Russian Dolls metaphor helps us to understand that a leader's personal journey never exists in isolation; it is surrounded by multiple other journeys occurring concurrently. When the journeys are aligned, something magical can happen.

We met Chris, the Asia-Pacific CEO of an Italian eyewear and eye care company, very briefly in the Coach chapter. I have only known Chris for a short time, but his has been one of the fastest journeys of transformation that I have ever witnessed. I put this down to Chris's sheer commitment and tenacity to "go fast and hard." But since Chris is one of our most recent case studies and he experienced our most fully realized version of the seven metaphors, his story is a testament to how transformation may be accelerated through their systematic use. What is so striking about Chris's rapid acceleration is that I could tell his story from a number of other angles. I could talk about the incredible journey of his business as a whole. Or I could talk about any one of the individual journeys taking place among his team members. I could talk about the transformation Chris has undergone on a very personal level, or the fact that he is now having an impact on a global stage with his story. I don't want to tell you any of the above stories in isolation; rather, I will endeavor to share a holistic story that draws all of them together, like a complete set of Russian dolls that fit neatly inside one another.

When I met Chris a year and a half ago, I could immediately empathize with his personal story. Like me, Chris had had a humble upbringing by loving and hard-working parents who taught him a strong work ethic and respect for the opportunities that were given to him. He made his way through the public education system, a task made much more enjoyable by his love of sports. You could say he tumbled into the eyewear industry when he was fresh out of university, taking the entry-level role of apprentice optical mechanic, where he learned the technical process of how to make eyeglasses. This was only ever meant to fill a gap year as he contemplated what to do with his studies, but he liked the environment and sensed a chance for an interesting career. With his eyes opened (pun intended) to new possibilities, he put himself through a part-time course of study to gain a business and economics degree. At the same time, he worked his way through different parts of the business, first in marketing, then human resources, and then operations. In 2004, he was promoted to COO, and in 2006 he was named CEO.

The promotion was an incredibly proud moment for Chris; he had worked his way up from the bottom. And his progression to the top position aligned with the company's overall performance. The organization was riding on the wave of a very effective scaling strategy that had made them the dominant player in the market—they had essentially gobbled up most of their big competitors. During the years Chris had been in the COO role, he had led the acquisition of his company's second-, third-, fourth-, and fifth-ranked competitors, so he felt he was in a very strong position going into the CEO job. On the back of these acquisitions, and with a large and loyal customer base, Chris played a key role in expanding his organization from three hundred fifty stores to a thousand in just a few years. It was an exciting time to be at the helm of the business, and Chris was determined to lead the organization to even higher levels of performance in the years ahead.

But, of course, this wouldn't be a story of transformation if everything went perfectly well from start to finish—in fact, it wouldn't be a story at all! Not long after Chris became CEO, his organization experienced the first of two seismic shifts. The onset of the global financial crisis in 2008 rattled consumer confidence and hit the retail part of the business pretty hard. And then, just as they were finding their feet again, they were faced with an even bigger challenge: a very aggressive, low-cost competitor that capitalized on consumers' reduced discretionary spending for luxury items, going from zero to a hundred thirty stores in its first twelve months. Chris and his team responded with their own budget offering but, in truth, this just confused their strategy. On top of these two very big issues, Chris also had to figure out how to take advantage of rapid growth in the Asian market.

I often say that it is comparatively easy to be an effective leader when times are good, but in the face of real challenges, a leader's true impact is revealed. These challenges really stung Chris, but they also solidified his intent: "To be in the business for so long as a successful leader, and then to take two big hits with the financial crisis and a very aggressive competitor — it wasn't a nice feeling to be the leader that presided over those issues, to be honest. It hurt a lot, and it wasn't the legacy I wanted to leave. I was determined to lead the business through these challenges in a way that built capability inside our organization so that we would never have to go through this kind of pain again."

This mix of pain and ambition was the foundation for our shared transformation agenda. Chris summarized his strategy for the company as "simplify, focus, and connect." This meant removing anything that got in the way of delivering exceptional customer service, consolidating the large array of brands they had built and acquired into two "super brands," and connecting with their customers on an emotional level. When I asked Chris how fast he wanted to move in pursuit of his agenda and how many layers of the organization he wanted to involve, it was like waving a red cape at a bull. Chris wanted "all of the dolls" aligned to his vision, including his executive team, his extended leadership team (direct reports of his executive team), the managers of his retail stores, and their teams. Together, they would drive the change as a united group — and they would need to do so quickly.

As you will have guessed by now, Chris had a huge appetite for change, and rapid change at that. But despite his very noble intentions for the organizational journey, he wasn't going about lining up his dolls in a very constructive fashion. He faced challenges with respect to his leadership style, which manifested itself in some rather aggressive and controlling behaviors.

"A day in my life then was 'Here's our plan — and I intricately want to be involved in every aspect of it,'" Chris explained later. "I guess I felt comfortable with pushing people to think bigger and go faster in order to achieve great performance. And I was reasonably good at doing that! But to be quite frank, I was giving everyone stress, imposing on their jobs, not giving them space — which is the furthest impact from what I wanted to have. I think it was the enormous pressure I was feeling, and the knowledge that I needed to move this thing — quickly."

Very early into our engagement, my colleague Ian and I challenged Chris about his impact, and how it was inhibiting his ambitions — which he acknowledged very readily. We encouraged him to take some of his hands-on energy and redirect it into creating an environment where his people could step up and take ownership of his agenda.

One of the first initiatives Chris undertook with his team was to create an emotionally engaging story about where the organization was headed and how they were going to get there. The goal was for every one of his eight thousand staff to understand their contribution to the journey ahead. In order to appeal to the hearts and minds of his people, he chose to present the story of how the organization would "simplify, focus, and connect" creatively, using a three-minute animation.

Despite the creative medium, it wasn't a glamorous task. Simplifying and refocusing the business meant that some people would lose their jobs. A lot of work went into communicating these messages authentically and sensitively. It's important to note that the storytelling was not outsourced to human resources or his communications team; it was always presented by Chris or a member of his executive team in face-to-face forums. What's more, it wasn't merely story "telling"; it was collaborative in nature. There were plenty of opportunities for staff to ask questions and contribute ideas toward the strategy. Rather than pushing the strategy onto his people, Chris was appealing for support and sharing ownership of the journey.

Chris and his team also shared the story with stakeholders beyond his region in an attempt to get greater alignment between his agenda and theirs. He knew he would struggle to be successful without their understanding and support, so this became a real focus for him.

"We showed other people who were going to be affected by our journey, including our suppliers and our global colleagues," Chris recalled later. "We put the animation on our global intranet so people all around the world could understand what was happening in our business, in just three minutes. We gave them an opportunity to offer input and feedback through a short survey, and that has triggered discussions all around the world."

With the strategy set and his people engaged, it became very obvious to Chris that leadership had to be the next big focus in the transformation effort. The strategy required that leaders all the way down to the store level enable employees to deliver an exceptional customer experience. So Chris committed his top four layers of management to an intensive journey of team and leadership transformation.

Every time Chris spoke about the leadership journey, he connected it to the organizational story. As a result, his four layers of management could see a very clear connection between their day-to-day role and the business's overarching goals. They understood that, as a team, they were leading the change.

All the while, the very process of engaging his organization was helping Chris shift his own impact as a leader. He had always been highly driven and achievement-oriented, but sometimes at the expense of the relational aspects of leadership. Now, he got better and better at creating a context for others to be successful, coaching and supporting them toward their goals.

"Nowadays, it's rare that anyone will walk out of my office saying 'I am not clear what the goal is, or what role each of us plays in achieving that goal,'" Chris later explained. "We now spend as much time as necessary to understand our expectations of one another, and how I can help my team to be successful. And I have found that this approach actually drives more of the edginess I was looking for, because things are clearer and people aren't confused. It's also given me back loads of time!"

This last point has been a revelation for Chris: the more he supports his people by being clear and creating a context for their success, the more time he has and the faster the organization goes. Not that long ago, Chris was known for having too many priorities, and wanting everything done by yesterday. Now he focuses all of his energy on what he calls the game-changers — the few actions that will make the biggest impact. Everyone in his organization knows now that if something is not on his game-changer list, he will delegate or eliminate it. As a result, he has more time than ever to coach his people toward higher levels of performance. It's a simple idea that has had a profound impact on Chris — and not just professionally.

Chris's leadership journey inspired him to go deeper than the leadership doll level and pay much greater attention to what we might call his personal doll. Chris realized that over several very hectic years, he had increasingly neglected his health.

"I guess as a result of the business pressures, it certainly hit me at a number of levels," Chris later told me. "With three lovely kids, I didn't want to be the guy who worked through his life and had a heart attack at fifty — and I was a good candidate. I'm someone who used to be pretty fit, so I don't think I was holding myself to the right standard. I felt misaligned with my values. So I dealt with that and got on the right foot. I now wake up at four every morning and exercise every day. It's my time and it is about getting fitter and healthier so I have the energy for life."

Chris was also inspired to refocus on his most important relationships: "My family and I do a couple of things together every week — whether we go out together or exercise together on a weekend. I'm very intentional about this now. It's critical that these relationships are really healthy as well."

As I said earlier, this is one of the fastest leadership transformations I have ever seen, and it goes to show what can happen when journeys are neatly aligned across an organization. Even at this early stage, the outcomes that are being achieved by Chris and his teams are nothing short of amazing. The leadership effectiveness of Chris and his fellow leaders has improved dramatically. They finished the last financial year with double-digit profit growth, which is close to double that of the previous year. This is a remarkable feat considering it's still early days and they are operating in the most difficult retail environment for decades.

Not surprisingly, the organizational results have created a stir up the line in Chris's environment. Chris's boss — the global CEO — was aware that Chris had embarked on a transformation agenda and was regularly given updates of progress along the way. As the results have shown up in the bottom line, the up-line interest has intensified: "My global CEO is very interested in our journey — in how we are thinking differently about our business and doing some things that aren't happening in other parts of the world. More and more, he is sending people my way, saying, 'Talk to Chris, understand what he is doing.'"

If this is only the first chapter in Chris's journey, then I'm really excited to see what comes next. For me, Chris's story is a powerful illustration of what becomes possible when leaders create very explicit links between their own journey and the journeys of those who accompany them. His story also points to the power of storytelling to create such linkages. What Chris's story is *not*, however, is a story of leadership transformation in isolation. To explore this observation more fully, I want to draw attention to two struggles my colleagues and I observed early on in our research, specifically when we asked our subjects, "What are the key factors that enabled you to transform?"

The first struggle was an inability in our research subjects to separate their own leadership journey from those of their teams and their organization as a whole. Eventually we stopped trying to maintain this separation and instead began exploring the interconnections between these journeys. This is the dolls-within-dolls application of the Russian Dolls metaphor.

Their second struggle was to articulate their transformation stories with any kind of color and depth. I knew firsthand how dramatic and compelling the stories of the leaders I had already worked with for many years were. In fact, this was a huge factor in my decision to undertake my doctoral research in the first place. But in their early reflections on their respective transformations, these leaders really struggled to communicate that drama. When I asked them to express their journeys through metaphor, a whole world of detail and insight opened up—and I will share this powerful experience later in this chapter.

Dolls-within-dolls

The concept of dolls-within-dolls arose from the multiple journeys we encountered in our original research that went above and beyond the leadership journey. In fact, the word "journey" was used so many times by leaders in their interviews that, quite frankly, it played havoc with the first round of data.

At the time, we found this incredibly frustrating. While we were trying to isolate the leadership journey, the leaders we were studying were speaking interchangeably about several different journeys that they were part of, so much so that we felt the integrity of our research was at risk. We tried to see how we could separate out the leadership journey specifically. After a while, though, it felt artificial to attempt such a feat, so we turned this problem on its head; rather than trying to artificially separate the journeys, we embraced interconnectedness as a way to shine a light on an important factor in how leaders transform.

Even in the very early stages of our research, clear patterns were emerging around the interconnectedness of three journeys in particular: the leadership journey, the team journey (for example, a leader's executive team, and sometimes their broader senior leadership group, such as the top hundred managers), and the organizational journey. As we started to explore the linkages explicitly, the leaders in turn reconfirmed that the journeys were indeed so intertwined that they could not separate them.

I first met Owen when he was building manager at a publicly listed construction company—a key member of the executive team reporting to a new general manager. In 2006, when my company's services were engaged by the GM, the business was underperforming across a range of financial, client, and safety indicators. The parent company was demanding a turnaround, but this was hampered by an organizational culture that was quite defensive and siloed across three operating divisions. Senior leaders were spending the majority of their time "doing" rather than leading the business toward a different future.

The senior team recognized they needed to transform the organization, and they were all committed to making the necessary changes. Owen's openness and warmth made him instantly likeable, and right from the beginning, he was excited about our working together. But likeability and commitment weren't going to be enough — it was clear that he needed to grow his leadership effectiveness if he was to realize his ambitions for his part of the business. Owen had spent his entire career in an industry notorious for its aggressive, adversarial nature and had internalized many of the negative traits of leaders who thrived in that world.

Fast-forward seven years, and I can tell you that Owen has made such a positive shift that he now occupies the general manager role himself, something even he considered a long shot back then. The data we have on the shift in Owen's effectiveness — four separate measures in seven years — is nothing short of impressive. It reveals a leader successfully inspiring his team to achieve individual and collective goals and to work effectively as a team, never mind the transformation in the business results, including dramatic revenue growth and industry leadership in safety.

With a before-and-after story like this, you might say that this is a great example of leadership transformation; that this person is worthy of study. You would want to know what happened in the middle of the story—how Owen made the shift. This was the position I found myself in at the outset of my doctoral research: I had a pool of leaders with incredible before-and-after stories. Initially, I assumed (and hoped) that my research would reveal eight to ten common factors that helped them become more effective leaders, and result in something of a recipe for transformation. But, as we will see, Owen's story only makes sense in the context of the journeys that surrounded his, that is, only if we look at all of the other dolls. His journey of leadership transformation is nested within one of the longest case studies of organizational transformation that I have been involved in—seven years and counting. So now to the middle part of that story.

When we commenced our journey together, it was, first and foremost, at the top level: the organizational doll. Owen's predecessor had engaged my firm to help them articulate their aspirations, develop a scorecard to measure progress toward those aspirations, and construct a story that could engage their diverse workforce in the future of the business.

Owen's boss was already a highly constructive leader, and he realized that company culture and leadership would be key drivers of the organizational outcomes he was looking for. We completed this first phase of work together by taking a measure of the operating culture, which revealed a workplace that valued aggressive and critical behaviors above all else. It became evident to all of us pretty quickly that if the organization was to transform its performance, the leaders would need to encourage a very different set of behaviors. So, in effect, we shifted our focus from the organizational doll to the executive team doll.

This shift meant that Owen, his peers, and his boss all had to sign up for a leadership journey of their own—the individual leadership doll. This involved a structured process of 360-degree assessment, qualitative peer feedback, and group and individual action planning. After six months of this work, the executive team moved on to the next doll, what we might call the extended leadership team doll, comprising the forty direct reports of the executive team.

Owen and the other executive members played a big role in getting the extended leadership team aligned to their strategic agenda. They agreed on clear measures of success for everyone, and these were aligned to the business goals we had developed earlier. They asked everybody to sign up for one of six big projects that came out of the business planning process. And they coached them, as well as held them accountable, for the action plans they developed following an assessment of their leadership effectiveness.

Over time, the extended leadership team stepped up and took on many of the responsibilities that the executive team had previously held, which in turn allowed the executive team to step into a more strategic role. Where once these executives had been tightly managing the business operations and reacting to crises, now they were spending more and more time setting the course and managing external stakeholders.

When Owen's boss elected semiretirement and moved into a corporate role, Owen was the natural choice to replace him as GM. And while he'd taken the reins from a very constructive leader, he wanted to put his own stamp on the organization. Specifically, he wanted to raise the level of accountability, as there was evidence that leaders at the top of his organization did not deal effectively with poor performance in their subordinates. He did this primarily by personally engaging in tough performance conversations that sent a clear message about the new expectations. His leadership story is about how he navigated these tensions constructively, and established accountability in more and more of the organization's dolls.

The longer Owen's journey has gone on, the more transformation has accelerated across his organization. This is no coincidence; Owen, his executive team, and his extended leadership team have each been able to see how their journey was aligned with the bigger picture, the organizational doll. All efforts at transformation by Owen and his colleagues were undertaken in the context of the organizational doll.

Through Owen's story, we have discovered four of the dolls in the set: the leadership doll, two layers of team dolls (the executive team and the extended leadership team), and the organizational doll. But there are at least two more very important dolls to consider, and they will grant us some of our most powerful insights yet into leadership transformation.

The up-line doll

The first additional doll that we found was that of the up-line environment; this might be an international parent company, a board of directors, or a state or federal regulatory body. Within the metaphor of the Russian Dolls, this constitutes the largest or outermost doll. What I find fascinating is that there have been markedly different experiences and interactions with the up-line doll for the leaders you've met in this book. Sometimes this big doll fit neatly around the smaller dolls, sometimes it fit loosely, but at other times it seemed that it had the capacity to squash all the others—and the leadership agenda with it. Additionally, the leaders' strategies for managing the up-line doll varied greatly, depending on their circumstances and their individual skill at this rather complex and nuanced task. One thing I've learned for certain is that the up-line doll has a very big impact on the speed and depth at which transformation can happen.

Given this range of experiences, it doesn't make sense for me to try to elaborate on the up-line doll with only one leader's experience. Instead, I will bring back a number of leaders we have met in previous chapters to illustrate the different scenarios they encountered, and offer strategies that can be employed to align—or at least neutralize—the up-line doll.

First, starting with a very positive scenario, I return to Tim—the young-gun advertising exec whom we met in the Fire and Coach chapters. For Tim, the up-line doll was a great enabler for his journey. His company's chairman was a great believer in the principles most commonly associated with a constructive approach to leadership—achieving great things, fostering innovation, and encouraging high levels of collaboration. He shared Tim's passion for worthy social causes, and was a key driver of the Earth Hour initiative. This intentional alignment on Tim's part between his leadership doll and his up-line doll was a key factor in Tim's successful transformation.

A more neutral scenario, in which the up-line doll was neither an enabler nor a hindrance, was what Clynton encountered. He was the capable but exhausted managing director of the skin-care and beauty giant whom we met in the Snowball and Movie chapters. Clynton's global parent company operated with a fairly decentralized structure so that he had sufficient autonomy to advance his leadership journey. Since Clynton's business was performing well, he was pretty much left alone to do his own thing. Consequently, his leadership agenda never came under any direct threat, and Clynton has been able to sustain it throughout multiple levels of his organization for eight years and counting.

Sometimes, though, the up-line doll can be a real hindrance, or worse still, it can threaten the other dolls. Here, I return to Paul, the six-foot-eight managing director of a Dutch IT subsidiary who was trying to fix a big gap in performance. Paul's up-line environment included a global CEO who used the metaphor of a baseball bat to describe his preferred style of leadership. Complicating matters further, his regional boss tried to kill off Paul's leadership journey altogether based on the company's poor performance. Paul and his team hung on to the other dolls for dear life, and managed to salvage their leadership agenda by demonstrating that this agenda was a pathway to growth. Once financial performance took a positive turn, Paul's up-line doll became very supportive of his leadership journey.

But it doesn't always turn out like a fairy tale, as was the case for Alan — the CEO of the German chemical and pharmaceutical company who "found religion" in the leadership-culture-performance link. Alan was so enthusiastic about the great work his company was doing locally, and the results he was getting, that he wanted his global superiors to join him on the journey. Metaphorically speaking, he was trying to fit the outermost doll into his smaller dolls. Unfortunately for Alan, this was met with the inevitable pain that the metaphor suggests; headquarters didn't share his enthusiasm for a change in the culture of the organization globally, and eventually they agreed to part ways.

When confronted with this difficult last scenario, I have learned that there are several effective strategies for managing the up-line doll in a way that at least protects the leadership agenda. The first is buying enough time for the lagging indicators, such as financial performance, to positively change. The best example of this is Mike, the CEO of the U.S. IT outsourcing company from the Fire and Mask chapters. Mike not only received the worst leadership feedback I had ever seen, but the financial performance of his company was also poor right from his first month in the role. Understandably, he feared his up-line doll would not approve of the large investment of time and money he was making in his transformation agenda when the short-term financial performance was so poor.

Rather than try to align his superiors with his leadership agenda, Mike kept a low profile on the investment he was making until he could demonstrate a tangible impact on the numbers, which happened about eighteen months in. Following this positive turn, when executives from headquarters came to visit, they would report back that "it feels different here." Over time, this resulted in a pull from Mike's up-line doll to better understand the leadership initiatives that were producing such great outcomes. In a very unlikely twist to Mike's story, his bosses too became engaged in a similar leadership journey, and Mike is now revered as something of a leadership guru across the corporation; this is no mean feat when you consider his first awkward steps in the role.

Often, a leader doesn't have the luxury of time or distance from headquarters and must confront potential dissent right up front. This was the case for Jim, the highly revered government director general who successfully led his organization through two massive crises, Cyclone Larry and an outbreak of equine influenza. As a senior public servant, Jim was subject to enormous scrutiny from the opposition party. Jim's leadership journey was sustained over time only because his boss — the government's minister for primary industries — was willing and able to defend it in Parliament against attacks from the opposition party. Jim's strategy was to equip the minister with a coherent story about how the leadership agenda fit very neatly with the government's agenda, and the promises that the government had made to its constituents regarding responsive and effective government.

A third strategy is to proactively test for support from the up-line doll before formally implementing the leadership agenda. This was the strategy used by Sylvia, the Australian managing director of a leading American fast-moving consumer goods company whom we met in the Snowball and Movie chapters. Before Sylvia and I began working together, she outlined to her boss her reasons for wanting to begin this journey, being very specific about how this would help her deliver on his most important outcomes of strong financial performance, halting market share decline, increasing customer advocacy, and encouraging a highly committed workforce. She then asked me to meet with her boss so that he could raise any questions or concerns. We agreed that he would be a key stakeholder in the journey, and that the three of us would meet once a quarter to discuss progress toward the agreed outcomes. At our second scheduled session, two quarters in, he opened our conversation with "Let me start by saying, I have never seen such a dramatic transformation so quickly in all of my professional life." Those were his exact words. No doubt his excitement was fueled by exceptional financial results that showed an increase in market share for the first time in ten years. But in large part it was the result of great work from Sylvia early on to involve him in the process and align her outcomes with his.

Wherever possible, I encourage leaders to follow Sylvia's path and align outcomes with their up-line doll right from the start. Where this is not possible, preparing a ready defense, as Jim did, or keeping a low profile, the way Mike did, can work very effectively. Whichever strategy you choose, I have learned that alignment between the up-line doll and the leadership agenda is a critical aspect of how leaders transform.

The personal doll

The final doll we revealed was the very personal journey that appeared to sit within each CEO's leadership journey. The leaders we studied seemed to use the terms "leadership journey" and "personal journey" interchangeably when they spoke about their transformations. But when I investigated this more deeply, they began to articulate distinctions between the two.

For some of the leaders in this book, the leadership doll encouraged them to make changes to their personal doll. We heard earlier in this chapter how Chris got his inner doll more aligned by getting fit and healthy again. Tim is another great example of this kind of alignment: "At the same time I was going through my leadership journey, I really developed a deep connection with yoga. And so the meditation, the integration of physical and mental and spiritual health, the way it teaches you a personal centeredness, turned out to be a massive influence. Losing a lot of weight, getting fit, getting healthy, getting organized — attempts to master these sorts of things were an important part of my transformation journey."

Sylvia and Clynton decided to change personal relationships that weren't serving them. Jim committed to more constructive relationships with his teenage kids after realizing that his authoritarian parenting style didn't sit well with his values — and didn't work particularly well either. Alan was determined to create a sense of balance between his work and home life so that he could prioritize his young family: "It was quite an awakening. I started to develop an awareness of my own physical well-being as well as the need to keep myself balanced in life. I realized I was spending too much time in the office, worrying about things that I couldn't fix, and making myself available twenty-four/seven whenever the people from Germany wanted something. And then I had the confidence to say, 'Hell no, just because it's ten A.M. there doesn't mean that you can ring me at eight P.M. here. I can't be effective. I'm just putting my little daughter to bed, so please don't ring me at that time.'"

One of my favorite expressions of the Russian Dolls metaphor, and the innermost, personal doll in particular, comes from Geoff, the young and irreverent managing director in the leading publicly listed food company, whom we met in the Movie chapter. As we heard in Geoff's story, he was all "go-go-go" at work, and was equally giving at home and in his community. But he realized that he was paying his personal doll no attention at all. He decided that if he was to transform his leadership and increase his overall happiness, he needed to "repaint his inner doll": "I started by looking at the things that I personally got enjoyment out of, which were also complementary to many other important aspects of my life. That's given way to a more interesting relationship with my wife, because I think she was going through the same sort of thing. We were both great parents, very active in the community, lots of outward giving and generosity, but exhausted at home. It was really re-energizing for us to focus on our inner dolls together."

These stories demonstrate how leaders can use what they learn in the professional realm to improve their personal lives. They reveal how you can use the leadership doll to effect positive change in your personal doll. The relationship between the dolls sometimes works the other way around, too: leaders can turn to the personal doll for inspiration for their leadership. Let's return to the story of Jim, who was a highly spiritual member of the ancient Syro-Malabar Christian faith. At the same time, in the early days of his leadership, Jim behaved like a Special Forces commando at work and didn't care who he stepped on to get the top result. His journey was about bringing more of the qualities of his personal doll into the leadership space: authenticity, disciplined reflection, and a community spirit. And if we look at Mike, on a personal level, he was a warm and good-humored family man; at work, he was awkward, distant, and switched between Mr. Aggressive and Mr. Passive. A key part of his leadership journey was connecting with the positive qualities he expressed with his family and bringing them to the fore at work.

No matter which way you look at it, when leaders connect with their personal doll—the innermost doll in the set—their journey of transformation can be accelerated. This truly reinforced my earlier research finding—that there is more joy to be found in searching for connections between the dolls than attempting to isolate and segment them. My friend Meg Wheatley speaks of this concept of wholeness in her groundbreaking book, *Leadership and the New Science: Discovering Order in a Chaotic World*: "We are refocusing on the deep longings we have for community, meaning, dignity, purpose, and love in our organizational lives. We are beginning to look at the strong emotions of being human, rather than segmenting ourselves by believing that . . . feelings are irrelevant in the organization."

Painting a story on the dolls

Earlier in this chapter, I said that there were two struggles that led us to conceive of the Russian Dolls metaphor: the struggle for leaders to separate their own leadership journey from the other journeys that surrounded them, which we just explored; and the struggle for leaders to give their transformation stories color and depth. This is what I want to talk about now.

When asked to give a rational and logical account of their journey, leaders are often quite stymied and stilted, as I found out in my very first research interview. I had picked Tim to go first because I felt he would be very animated and articulate in his responses to my questions, for a number of reasons: his outgoing personality, his creative background, and my recollections of the many colorful incidents in his journey. Suffice it to say that the interview fell well short of my expectations, and his. Tim's answers left out many of the memorable incidents I remembered. They were also very dry and lacked the profound insights I had experienced with him many times before.

It was only when I turned off the tape recorder and expressed my frustration to Tim that our interview suddenly burst into life. Tim told me that his stiltedness was a result of his struggle with the notion that he had transformed. He said that if leadership transformation was a martial art, he had only progressed from white belt to yellow belt: "I'm still integrating the principles and concepts of effective leadership into my day-to-day interactions. So I'd like to get to the point where this nice constructive style becomes like breathing, but I doubt I'll ever get there. It's like any art; I think there's a journey. I'm really glad that I've become a yellow belt, and I'm looking forward to becoming a black belt."

This spoke profoundly to me, particularly compared to the rest of Tim's interview. It really helped to capture the essence of Tim's journey. Tim allowed people to see him for who he was, good and bad. His journey was imperfect, yet genuine and inspiring to others. And as far as Tim was concerned, his journey was far from complete — and never would be.

To my delight, there was a similar explosion of color and clarity from all of the leaders in this book when they expressed their experiences through metaphor. What I find very interesting is that, even though each leader employed a similar framework of tools, milestones, and interventions, they all arrived at very different interpretations of their journeys. This confirms to me how much transformation is bound by the unique context and experience of the leader. On closer inspection, however, there appear to be some common themes in the metaphors they used, which I find complementary to many of the lessons I've shared in earlier parts of this book.

The first common theme is that of gradual metamorphosis, that is, a progression from one state to another over time. This was illustrated in Tim's notion of progressing to different belts in the martial arts. Clynton offered the following metaphor: "I could compare it to the process that leaves go through in autumn. It is a gradual change of color, hardly noticeable each day, but if you look at where they start and where they finish, it is dramatic and it is a really pretty picture." Mike put it another way: "I can look back now and joke about my initial feedback. It was some of the worst results that they had seen in the history of CEOs. It was a horror story. The change and transformation journey I went on was very satisfying and gratifying. The change I saw in front of me was more than statistically significant, it was visually significant. It feels like going from ugly duckling to a swan — it was a bit of a fairy tale, really."

A second common theme that emerged from the leaders' metaphors was the idea of an awakening. Christine offered the following metaphor: "Leadership is extremely hard work and, as leaders, we face many barriers — but I discovered over time that most of those barriers were in my head. It was like I was sleep-walking, and then I woke up." Sylvia talked about discovering new parts of a house: "It feels a bit like restoring an old building. I was comfortable with what I had, but on closer inspection I realized the house was full of dust and junk. As I cleaned it out I found cupboards and rooms that I didn't know about. They needed a really good sorting and cleaning and some needed major modifications. As this spreads through the organization it is like a whole neighborhood developing — including a real sense of camaraderie. And I have a strong sense that the discovery will continue."

The final common theme that emerged from the leaders' metaphors was the concept of navigating varied terrains in pursuit of a destination, clumsily at first, but with more and more finesse and grace over time. Jim compared it quite beautifully to the seventeenth-century Christian allegory *The Pilgrim's Progress*: "There's the land of success ahead, where you can experience a synchronized universe, where your purpose, outcomes, relationships, and structures, systems and capabilities are fully aligned. You're making a difference, but you're part of a community making a difference, and you are fully aligned both personally and in your work. There isn't a dichotomy that exists between Jim the family man and Jim the working person — they're one and the same person. And you can be yourself one hundred percent and not have to role-play. In *The Pilgrim's Progress*, there are a number of challenges and dangerous ravines to cross and enemies that you face and times that you think you are going to die, you're going to fall off these cliffs or bridges that look very fragile. But it's your profound belief in where you're going that keeps you on the path, and the only difference that I've learnt now is that the pilgrim's progress is actually there at every moment, it's not an end point, it's actually there each time that you move, and each time it becomes clearer, because it was always there — it waited for you to open your eyes and see it."

Alan put it another way: "At the beginning, it looks like stress, lack of direction, groping around in the dark. It's midnight, there's no moon, you're in a jungle, there are swamps around, you've got a rough idea of where you want to go but you've got no compass. Later in the journey, the sun is shining and you're feeling pretty damn good about yourself because you've put things in place. The biggest thing on this journey is, you move from not knowing to knowing about yourself, and it's the realization on that journey that if you want change, the first thing that's got to change is yourself. You've got to have a damn hard look at yourself. Standing outside of yourself and looking back at yourself as though you are seeing yourself replayed on video is very powerful. So the picture I paint is going from darkness into light. It sounds a bit over the top, but that's how I feel."

Finally, Dennis put it this way: "I can picture in my mind going from a beginner to an experienced snow skier. And it just seems to me that actually articulates the journey quite well. You start off snow ploughing and you have to put so much energy into achieving, relatively speaking, so little. And as you get better and better at skiing, you're putting far less energy into it, and you're achieving so much more. So you actually use all of the environment to your advantage; you're using the steepness of the mountain, you're using the amount of snow on the slopes, you're going down as quickly as you can in an exhilarating fashion, because you can use that terrain and you can use that environment to your advantage. I think when you start out on the leadership journey, it's really hard because it's scary; you're not sure how people are going to react to it. And if you start using the environment to your advantage, you start to realize people really want to be led — they want to see that the business has a future. And if you can give them that, you've freed up all their energies, that'll make the rest of your life so much easier to cope with."

My work has really opened my mind to the power of metaphors for generating insights into how leaders transform. Beyond the obvious benefit of adding color and richness to the research, I have found the process of generating metaphors to describe transformation to be incredibly useful for leaders as they try to reflect and make sense of their journey. Metaphors can assist leaders to access memories and insights that otherwise might not be available to them. In addition, they are powerful devices for engaging others in their leadership journey, and sharing metaphors with others can lead to new insights and themes.

Now what?

If you're action oriented or ready to start getting your Dolls lined up, then I suggest you go to www.peterfuda.com and interact with the Russian Dolls audiovisual tools and exercises before coming back to read the next chapter. If you would prefer to keep reading, or you're not ready for any deep reflection yet, then here are a couple of simple next steps:

- Consider how many of the six dolls are relevant to your leadership journey.
- Reflect on how aligned your personal journey is with the imperatives of your leadership role.
- Think about how you could better align your up-line doll to your journey.
- Reflect on what metaphor best describes your journey to date, and whether this is the same metaphor you would like for your journey in the future.

Conclusion

I N T H I S B O O K, I have introduced you to seven interdependent metaphors: Fire (ambition), Snowball (accountability and momentum), Master Chef (frameworks, tools, and
strategies), Coach (support and feedback), Mask (authenticity),
Movie (self-reflection), and Russian Dolls (coordinating multiple journeys). They were forged in the brutally honest reflections of a select group of successful leaders, and since then, my
colleagues and I have used them to explain, inspire, and accelerate leadership transformation in leaders at all levels, in all types
of organizations, all around the world; many of their stories
have also been included in this book.

I firmly believe that these seven metaphors represent a
unique method of addressing the fairly common challenge of
leadership transformation in a fresh and unconventional way.
I have not laid out a neat multistep model for change, nor am I
prescribing a magic pill that will turn the ordinary leader into a
superhero, and I'm unapologetic about that. Instead, I have offered seven metaphors that can be used creatively and fluidly
by leaders in ways that make sense in their particular context.

In essence, I am proposing a new type of change methodology where the leadership art is as important, or perhaps even more important, than the leadership science.

The enthusiasm with which leaders have embraced these metaphors has, quite frankly, caught me by surprise. Part of that enthusiasm, I believe, has less to do with my metaphors per se, and more to do with the power of metaphors in general. In my recent experiences of applying metaphors to leadership transformation, there are several things I have learned about why they work so well, which I would like to share with you in conclusion.

First and foremost, metaphors make complex stuff simple. We use a saying in my organization, given to me by another mentor: "If a picture is worth a thousand words, a metaphor is worth a thousand pictures." If I were to try to engage leaders in the theoretical basis for my approach to leadership transformation, I would be met with yawns or worse. On the other hand, I have to be careful not to oversimplify what can be deep and multifaceted lessons. These are both challenges leaders face every day. Metaphors fill the space in between these extremes — they invite people into the idea. It's much easier to explore the idea once you're inside it (yes, I just used a metaphor to explain the power of metaphor).

Taking this idea one step further, metaphors are about the audience, not the presenter. If I want to show you how clever I am, I can use complex concepts and management jargon. If I want to show you how much I care for you, I will park my self-importance for a little while and use a metaphor. It never ceases to amaze me how open and receptive senior leaders become when I go down this second path.

Metaphors are also powerful simply because they are familiar. I imagine that if I'd come up with a seven-step model for leadership transformation, people would find it hard to recount each step—even on a good day. And yet it seems very easy for leaders to remember and access these seven metaphors in their everyday work. Their familiarity means leaders can recall them easily, which is helpful when trying to change entrenched behavior—even when you're having a bad day. Their familiarity also allows leaders to talk about them effectively with a group. As the organizational theorist Karl Weick once wrote, "People see more things than they can describe in words."

In our work, almost daily I come across examples of how these seven metaphors have been used "artistically" by leaders as enablers of change in themselves and others—and this may be the most powerful of all the reasons to use them. Once a metaphor is articulated, the receiver, not the presenter, owns it. The receiver may interpret the metaphor in ways that are unique and important to him or her. To illustrate the point, recently I was delivering a talk on the Fire metaphor, and a very engaged audience member told me afterward that this talk had helped to "reignite" her passion for leadership and put a "fire in her belly" for the journey ahead—two unfoldings of the metaphor that I had not mentioned at all, and both of which made my day. Unlike models, formulas, and frameworks, metaphors

The 7 Metaphors for Leadership Transformation®

Research and Development by Dr. Peter Fuda. ©2010. All Rights Reserved

Figure 11

open rather than close thinking, they inspire rather than restrict creativity, and they encourage the listener to create alternative and complementary meanings.

While I have discussed the seven metaphors in seven separate chapters, I have hinted at their interdependencies throughout. These interdependencies are illustrated best in figure 11, showing all seven metaphors together.

In this context, I would like to emphasize two key insights.

First, all of the metaphors have a fluid relationship to one another in the process of leadership transformation. And second, the Fire is at the center of the seven metaphors because it provides the context, purpose, and leverage for the other six. As Nietzsche once said, "He who has a why to live can bear almost any how." Similarly, I have learned that if the fire goes out, all other factors are redundant.

I now invite you to make these metaphors your own. I encourage you to identify your own burning ambition, to create a snowball of accountability around your drive toward it, to create a tasty recipe of frameworks, tools, and strategies, to sign up a trusted coaching staff, to drop any masks that are preventing you from moving forward, to constantly review and edit your story as a movie director would, and to align your own leadership journey with the others that surround you. These seemingly simple prompts will support you in the kind of organized reflection and purposeful action that are the hallmark of highly effective leaders.

As I stated in the introduction of this book, to help you on your journey, my colleagues and I have designed a very comprehensive set of free resources on my blog. These resources include three-minute animations of each metaphor, documentary-style footage of many of the leaders in the book, and dozens of exercises that will allow you to put the metaphors into practice on your own or with your team. Until now, these resources have only been available to the clients of our management consultancy, so I'm excited to share them with you. To access these resources, simply go to my blog, www.peterfuda.com, and follow the prompts.

I'd love to hear about your experiences with the seven metaphors. You can contact me directly at peter@peterfuda.com.

Acknowledgments

"If I have seen a little further it is by standing on the shoulders of giants."

— ISAAC NEWTON

I'm writing these acknowledgments, the very last task before submitting this book to my publisher, on Tuesday, October 30th, 2012, in my Manhattan hotel room on the 42nd floor of the Trump Hotel in Soho. Some of you will have worked out the significance of this date: it's the day after Hurricane Sandy smashed the Northeast of the United States. Surveying the devastation to lower Manhattan and New Jersey from my window is quite a surreal and humbling experience. So was my experience last night as my room rocked two to three feet for several hours in pitch-black darkness.

OK, that was terrifying.

I'm not sure if it was feeling the awesome power of Mother Nature up close, experiencing the warmth of the hotel staff as they selflessly looked after their guests, or watching the courageous and committed emergency workers trying to get the city back on its feet from first light, but I woke up with Isaac Newton on my mind. I would like to acknowledge the many "giants" who have made this book—and the research it's based on—possible. I do so in the strong belief that this work simply would never have happened without them. This is not the work of a single, committed individual; it is the work of a powerful community sharing knowledge and support.

My wife, Kara, has contributed in countless ways. She has provided emotional support and has done the lion's share of parenting our beautiful daughter, Isabella—particularly as deadlines approached for my doctoral work and then for this book. She also got me through Quantitative Research Methods with the credits I needed to progress to the thesis, which ultimately transformed into this book. Thank you for your support and encouragement, Kara—I love you.

As the father of any little girl knows, a smile, a hug, or a kiss can provide the perspective and inspiration to keep you going in the face of any obstacle. So thank you, Bella, for the thousands of smiles, hugs, and kisses that kept me going—you're the greatest gift ever.

My mum and dad, Lina and Joe, my brother and sister, Mark and Melisa, have provided me with continuous encouragement and support for as long as I can remember. It was great to work with Mark on all of the audiovisual material that accompanies this book—Mark, I don't know where you got your creative skills from, but I'm glad you got them. I'd like to thank my mum in particular for instilling in me the values of self-reliance, account-ability, and resilience; these gifts have kept on giving throughout the last seven years of research and writing.

Thanks to my literary agent, Markus Hoffman, for your guid-ance, wise counsel, and friendship — not to mention the first edit of this book. Thanks to David Moldawer, Carmen Johnson, and the team at Amazon Publishing for believing so strongly in me — I hope you will be proven a good judge of talent! Similarly, thanks to Daniel Crewe and the team at Profile in the UK.

I am particularly grateful to the stars of this book: Alan, Geoff S., Vicki, Mike, Jim, Christine, Clynton, Anthony, Sylvia, Tim, Paul, Dennis, Chris, Geoff E., Liz, Owen, Bernie, and Ken. Your commitment, humility, and authenticity continue to be a source of inspiration to me and to all who are affected by your leadership. In large part, I dedicate this book to the memory of Liz, a wonderful young leader and beautiful human being who passed well before her time.

Professor Richard Badham was the best supervisor, mentor, and friend that I could have hoped for during my original doc-toral research process. I am very grateful for your commitment, wisdom, and feedback. I have no doubt that this work is infi-nitely better because of your guidance — thank you.

Thank you to Dr. Rob Cooke of Human Synergistics Interna-tional for your friendship, wise counsel, and for the small matter of pioneering the concept of a leader's impact some twenty years ago — you were ahead of your time.

A big thanks to James O'Toole and Chris Cheatley of the CEO Forum, John Karagounis of the CEO Circle, and Ray Weekes of the CEO Institute. The platforms that each of you provided to me and to the leaders in this study over the past few years forced us to get clear on our stories and insights well in advance of this book. It was a great discipline that I believe improved our work.

Thank you to my second family, the team at The Alignment Partnership: Johanna Jordan, Ian Moore, Graham Dunn, Ron Schwartz, Leanne Myers, Angie Virtue, Martin Lombard, Will Blunt, and Mancy Li. Your direct contributions to this study, as well as your friendship and support, have been of immense benefit to me. I also appreciate your keeping our business healthy and growing when my attention has been divided.

I have left Skye Phillips until last because her contribution to this work—doctoral thesis and book—has been simply immense. From the very start, you have played the roles of assistant, partner, confidante, supervisor, and pain in the backside—often all on the same day. Your commitment, insight, and intellect have improved this work immeasurably and for that I am eternally grateful.

Appendix

Why I Use the Leadership/Impact Tool

As I highlighted in "Read This First" at the start of this book, the leadership transformations we documented in our research were not just anecdotal; we captured quantitative data on these shifts using a 360-degree survey instrument called Leadership/Impact (a registered trademark of Human Synergistics International) developed by Dr. Robert Cooke, associate professor emeritus of Managerial Studies at the University of Illinois at Chicago and CEO of Human Synergistics International.

While leadership is a subjective and often intangible concept, the Leadership/Impact tool gives us a rigorous, non-biased means for "quantifying" transformation in a leader. Through our research, the Leadership/Impact tool also emerged as an important element of leadership transformation in its own right, as you will have read about in chapter three: Master Chef.

In case you're wondering, no, I do not have shares in Human Synergistics, nor will I profit in any way if you choose to purchase this tool. There are just a lot of reasons why I use it in the process of leadership transformation, which I'd like to be transparent about.

The Leadership/Impact tool has proven to be a reliable and valid measure of a leader's effectiveness, all around the world, for many years. This helps me to build trust with leaders so that they can move on quickly to acceptance and action, rather than get stuck in an intellectual debate about whether the data are valid.

It does not measure traits, personality, or even the behavior of an individual leader; rather, it measures a leader's impact, that is, how the leader *motivates and encourages others to behave.* As a result, I have found that defensive reactions to challenging feedback are not as frequent or intense as is the case with some other survey tools.

It employs a language that is familiar to senior leaders: "effectiveness," "impact," and "strategies" — all things that leaders care about. Its colors of blue, red, and green give leaders a language that they can use in everyday executive life. For example: "That wasn't very blue [Constructive]! I know you were trying to get to a better solution but your aggression made everyone go green [Passive-Defensive]."

Perhaps most importantly, the Leadership/Impact tool relies on a participant set vision or ideal impact, not an "expert" established benchmark. A Constructive Leadership/Impact is the one most desired by leaders. Consequently, I generally do not have to preach to leaders about the benefits of a Constructive impact; they will almost always tell me through their ideal impact profile that this is what they want.

As I showed in "Read This First," a leader's ideal impact is usually very different from his or her actual impact. When this gap appears in hard data, my job as a change agent is to support the leader to meet his or her own vision, rather than impose my viewpoint or theoretical expertise.

Leaders receive data on how they are using ten very well-researched leadership strategies to create their actual impact. If leaders desire to shift their impact, they can easily identify strategies that will be helpful in this pursuit.

Finally, I have found that the Leadership/Impact tool has the complexity that's required for credibility, but the simplicity that's required for action. The 100-page report, with its abundance of data points, gives leaders the comfort that they are holding something trustworthy and important—even if they never go through it in detail. But the two or three important pages that provide a picture of where leaders currently are, profiled against their aspiration, allow them to move to action quickly.

If you would like to get access to this tool, simply go to the Human Synergistics website, www.humansynergistics.com, and then select your country for the relevant contact details.

Sources

READ THIS FIRST

Decades of academic analysis have given us more than 350 definitions of leadership . . .

Bennis, Warren G. and Burt Nanus (1985). *Leaders: Strategies for Taking Charge.* New York: Harper & Row.

. . . given the often-quoted statistic that more than 70 percent of all change efforts end in failure . . .

Change failure statistic based on thirty years of leadership research by Dr. John Kotter, as referenced in http://www.kotterinternational.com/our-principles/changesteps/changesteps. The original research can be found in Kotter, John P. (1996), *Leading Change*, Boston, MA: Harvard Business School Press.

To paraphrase Karl Weick, we can only make sense of life retrospectively, even though it must be lived prospectively.

Weick, Karl E. (1979). *The Social Psychology of Organizing.* 2nd ed. Boston, MA: Addison-Wesley Publishing Company.

———. (1995). *Sensemaking in Organizations (Foundations for Organizational Science).* Thousand Oaks, CA; London; New Delhi: Sage Publications.

. . . this dream came true when HBR published "Fire, Snowball, Mask, Movie: How Leaders Spark and Sustain Change," based on our research findings.

Fuda, Peter A. and Richard Badham (2011). "Fire, Snowball, Mask, Movie: How Leaders Spark and Sustain Change." *Harvard Business Review* (November): 145–48.

. . . Richard and I had the good fortune to speak with leadership guru Manfred Kets de Vries following a lecture he gave in 2006.

Conducted at the Wesley Centre, Sydney. Organized by Macquarie Graduate School of Management.

. . . *inspired by Karl Weick's assertion that "people see more things than they can describe in words" . . .*

Weick, Karl E. (1998). *The Social Psychology of Organizing: Topics in Social Psychology.* 2nd ed. New York: McGraw-Hill.

Quantitative data on these shifts were captured by the 360-degree survey instrument we used with our leaders — Leadership/Impact

Cooke, Robert A. (1997). Leadership/Impact: Measuring the Impact of Leaders on Organizational Performance. Plymouth, MI: Human Synergistics.

FIRE

In early 2007, Tim became one of three founding directors on a new initiative called Earth Hour.

Earth Hour is an initiative that was jointly developed by World Wildlife Fund Australia and the advertising agency Leo Burnett Sydney in 2007 to raise awareness about the environment and global warming. For more information and statistics, see http://www.wwf.org.au/earthhour/.

It was management consultant Daryl Conner who first coined the concept of the burning platform . . .

Conner, Daryl R. (1993). *Managing at the Speed of Change: How Resilient Managers Succeed and Prosper Where Others Fail.* New York: Random House.

Kotter, John P. (1996). *Leading Change.* Boston, MA: Harvard Business School Press.

As Kotter explains in his book, Leading Change, *"Visible crises can be enormously helpful in catching people's attention and pushing up urgency levels."*

Kotter, John P. (1996). *Leading Change.* Boston, MA: Harvard Business School Press.

As Stephen R. Covey once said, "Motivation is a fire from within. If someone else tries to light that fire under you, chances are it will burn very briefly."

Covey, Stephen R. (1989). *The Seven Habits of Highly Effective People: Powerful Lessons in Personal Change.* New York: Free Press.

Daniel H. Pink, author of Drive: The Surprising Truth About What Motivates Us . . .

Pink, Daniel H. (2009). *Drive: The Surprising Truth About What Motivates Us.* 1st ed. New York: Riverhead.

Sources

SNOWBALL

My friend, the researcher and author Brené Brown, explains it like this in her book, Daring Greatly . . .

Brown, Brené (2012). *Daring Greatly: How the Courage to Be Vulnerable Transforms the Way We Live, Love, Parent, and Lead.* New York: Gotham.

MASTER CHEF

The concept of impact, as it relates to leadership, was pioneered by Dr. Robert Cooke . . .

Cooke, Robert A. (1997). Leadership/Impact: Measuring the Impact of Leaders on Organisational Performance. Plymouth, MI: Human Synergistics.

. . . the tool I used to baseline the impact of all of the leaders I'm discussing is a 360-degree measurement instrument . . .

Cooke, Robert A. (1997). Leadership/Impact: Measuring the Impact of Leaders on Organizational Performance. Plymouth, MI: Human Synergistics.

. . . scholars James Kouzes and Barry Posner speak about . . .

Kouzes, James M. and Barry Z. Posner (2012). *The Leadership Challenge: How to Make Extraordinary Things Happen in Organizations.* 5th ed. San Francisco, CA: Jossey-Bass.

In fact, the Leadership/Impact tool presents ten very well researched strategies.

Cooke, Robert A. (1997). Leadership/Impact: Measuring the Impact of Leaders on Organizational Performance. Plymouth, MI: Human Synergistics.

The five strategies that I outline below are based, in part, on my observation . . .

Cooke, Robert A. (1997). Leadership/Impact: Measuring the Impact of Leaders on Organizational Performance. Plymouth, MI: Human Synergistics.

. . . 93 percent of us believe we are above-average drivers!

Svenson, Ola (1981). "Are We All Less Risky and More Skillful than Our Fellow Drivers?" *Acta Psychologica* 47 no. 2 (February): 143–48.

A simple formula we use with leaders, adapted from American psychologist Norman R. F. Maier . . .

Maier's original equation was $E=Q{\times}A$, in: Maier, N.R.F. (1931). "Reasoning in Humans. II: The Solution of a Problem and Its Appearance in Consciousness." *Journal of Comparative Psychology* 12, no. 2: 181–94.

Sources

COACH

According to the Merriam-Webster Dictionary, *the word "coach" is derived from the Hungarian* kocsi, *a type of large wagon used to transport passengers.*

"coach." Merriam-Webster.com. 2010. http://www.merriam-webster.com (February 2010).

MASK

To explore the Mask of concealment, I'm going to talk about Andrew Lloyd Webber's The Phantom of the Opera.

The Phantom of the Opera (in French, *Le Fantôme de l'Opéra*) by Gaston Leroux was first published as a serialization in *Le Gaulois* from September 23, 1909, to January 8, 1910 (source: Amazon Books). The 1986 Andrew Lloyd Webber musical first opened in London's West End with Michael Crawford in the title role and Sarah Brightman as Christine Daaé.

To explore this second application of the Mask metaphor, let's turn to the 1994 Jim Carrey vehicle The Mask.

The Mask is a 1994 American fantasy/comedy film based on a series of comic books published by Dark Horse Comics. It was directed by Chuck Russell and produced by Dark Horse Entertainment and New Line Cinema, and originally released to theaters on July 29, 1994 (source: Wikipedia).

Brené Brown puts it beautifully in her book, Daring Greatly . . .

Brown, Brené (2012). *Daring Greatly: How the Courage to Be Vulnerable Transforms the Way We Live, Love, Parent, and Lead.* New York: Gotham.

The renowned management scholar Edgar Schein refers to this approach . . .

Schein, Edgar H. (1961). *Coercive Persuasion: A Socio-psychological Analysis of the "Brainwashing" of American Civilian Prisoners by the Chinese Communists.* New York: W. W. Norton.

Frances Hesselbein, one of the foremost contributors to leadership thinking . . .

United States Army (author), Frances Hesselbein and Eric K. Shinseki (introduction), and Richard E. Cavanagh (foreword). (2004). *Be Know Do: Leadership the Army Way; Adapted from the Official Army Leadership Manual.* San Francisco: Jossey-Bass.

MOVIE

Shakespeare gave us the metaphor of life as a stage in Jaques's famous monologue . . .

For the most prominent example, see work by sociologist Erving Goffman in
Goffman, Erving (1959). *The Presentation of Self in Everyday Life.* New
York: Doubleday.

*. . . they felt as though they were trapped in a repeating scenario — just
like Phil Connors, the Pittsburgh TV weatherman played by Bill Murray
in Harold Ramis's classic* Groundhog Day.

Screenplay written by Danny Rubin and Harold Ramis, based on a story by
Rubin. The comedy film was released in 1993. In 2006, the film was
added to the United States National Film Registry as being deemed cul-
turally, historically, or aesthetically significant.

*Our concept of the editing suite can be compared to organizational theo-
rist Donald Schön's notion of "reflection-on-action."*

Schön, Donald A. (1984). *The Reflective Practitioner: How Professionals Think in
Action.* New York: Basic Books.

RUSSIAN DOLLS

My friend Meg Wheatley speaks of this concept of wholeness . . .

Wheatley, Margaret J. (1994). *Leadership and the New Science: Discovering Order
in a Chaotic World.* San Francisco, CA: Berrett-Koehler Publishers.

CONCLUSION

*As the organizational theorist Karl Weick once wrote, "People see more
things than they can describe in words."*

Weick, Karl E. (1998). *The Social Psychology of Organizing: Topics in Social Psychology.* 2nd ed. New York: McGraw-Hill.

APPENDIX

*Leaders receive data on how they are using ten very well-researched lead-
ership "strategies."*

Cooke, Robert A. (1997). Leadership/Impact: Measuring the Impact of Leaders
on Organizational Performance. Plymouth, MI: Human Synergistics.

Index

Page numbers for illustrations are in italic type.